Marks in Place
Contemporary Responses to Rock Art

Marks in Place
Contemporary Responses to Rock Art

Photographs by Linda Connor
        Rick Dingus, Book Coordinator
        Steve Fitch
        John Pfahl
        Charles Roitz, Project Director

Essays by Polly Schaafsma and Keith Davis

Foreword by Lucy R. Lippard

University of New Mexico Press
Albuquerque

Library of Congress Cataloging-in-Publication Data

Marks in place.

  Bibliography: p.
  Contents: Rock art, ideas in time and space / Polly Schaafsma—Gestures of faith / Linda Connor—Places, dreams, and journeys / Rick Dingus—[etc.]
  1. Photography of art.   2. Rock paintings—United States—Pictorial works.
3. Petroglyphs—United States—Pictorial works.   I. Connor, Linda, 1944–
II. Schaafsma, Polly.   III. Davis, Keith F., 1952–
TR657.M36   1987   779′.97′090113   86-24965
ISBN 0-8263-0975-5
ISBN 0-8263-0976-3 (pbk.)

© 1988 by the University of New Mexico Press.
All rights reserved.
Second paperback printing, 1989

Contents

Acknowledgments	vii
Foreword, *Lucy R. Lippard*	ix
Rock Art, Ideas in Time and Space, *Polly Schaafsma*	1
Gestures of Faith, *Linda Connor*	7
Plates	13
Places, Dreams, and Journeys: Long-Term Contexts for Now and Later, *Rick Dingus*	33
Plates	39
About Being in Places, *Steve Fitch*	59
Plates	65
Elegy for the Drowned, *John Pfahl*	85
Plates	89
A Part of the Medium, *Charles Roitz*	97
Plates	100
Modernism and the Quest for Primacy, *Keith Davis*	121
About the Contributors	133

Acknowledgments

We would like to thank the many people and organizations who shared their research, gave of their time and ideas, or otherwise supported our efforts in this project as it evolved.

Early on the National Endowment for the Arts Photographic Survey Project "Marks and Measures: Pictographs and Petroglyphs in a Modern Art Context" was conceived, formulated, and written by Robin Grace and Charles Roitz. In this Robin deserves substantial credit, as she does also for her later fund-raising efforts and general support. William (Billy) Parker was most helpful as an advisor in selecting the photographers for the project. We are grateful for his good judgment. Without the original funding from the NEA very little would have been possible. Their contribution and faith in the creative process and in creative individuals cannot be given enough recognition. The University of Colorado at Boulder administered this effort with flexibility and generosity and also provided some direct financial aid through the Council on Research and Creative Work and the Rio Abiseo National Park Project. Payson Sheets and Tom Lennon were especially generous in their support. We thank them both and the university. The Institute for University Research at Texas Tech University also provided some direct financial aid, for which we are deeply grateful.

A project such as this owes something to the work of other photographers. Nathan Lyons and his interest in pictorial language systems must certainly be recognized here, as should the help that Gary Metz gave to the project.

A number of us have benefitted greatly from the important research of Polly Schaafsma, whose many books and articles on rock art not only led us to sites but also helped clarify our understanding of the relationships between marks and place. Our sincere appreciation goes to her for her scholarship, her encouragement, and the discussions we had that affected our orientation to the subject. We also thank Emanual Anati who shared his ideas about the global significance of rock art and Curtis Schaafsma for his useful information and good advice concerning rock art sites covered by New Mexico reservoirs.

A great many people helped guide us to actual rock art sites. We thank them all but would especially like to thank Mike Bilbo, Pete Laudeman, Slim Maberry, and Dave Parker for their substantial efforts at helping us find important places. Dan Budnik deserves our appreciation for sharing his ideas and knowledge of places and for introducing us to contemporary traditionals among the Hopi and Navajo of Arizona. A number of people also helped carry supplies or accompanied us into the field. Among them we thank Michelle Brown, David Carpenter, Stephen Federation, Billy Hare, Mark Klett, Lawrence McFarland, William S. Sutton, and Peter Warshall for their assistance and good spirits along the way. Actually, scores of people helped us with our physical burden of supplies and equipment in the field, but only a few were there for us both in the field and at home with helpful insights, valued encouragement, and intelligent, honest responses to the work in progress. Of this latter group, Lynn Grimes and Susan Renzo were indispensable and are very much appreciated.

We would like to thank everyone who has helped make it possible to exhibit our work and share it with the general public. Tom Southall first showed a portion of the project in conjunction with a symposium that he arranged at the University of Kansas at Lawrence in the spring of 1985. We thank Tom for his enthusiasm, professionalism, and the moral and financial support he provided by showing and collecting our work. Eric Paddock of the Colorado Historical Society also deserves our sincere appreciation for his major efforts at organizing a permanent archive and a traveling exhibition of this work. Bill Jenkins, too, deserves our gratitude for his early interest and advice concerning potential avenues for making our work accessible to a wider audience.

Finally, we wish to thank the writers who contributed to this book and helped illuminate the concerns of our project in various ways. Lucy Lippard we thank for her insightful discussion of our response from a contemporary perspective. Polly Schaafsma we thank once more for sharing her understanding of the archeological significance of rock art. Keith Davis we thank for his discussion of the fascination that primitivism has held for artists since the beginning of the modern era. Dana Asbury, our editor at UNM Press, we thank for her patience, her clarification of all the writing, and her help in creating this book you see before you.

Linda Connor
Rick Dingus
Steve Fitch
John Pfahl
Charles Roitz

There are still ancient
 symbols
  alive
I did dance with the prehistoric horse
years and births later
near a cave wall
last winter
. . . .
I am memory alive
 not just a name
but an intricate part
of this web of motion,
meaning: earth, sky, stars circling
my heart
centrifugal.

—Joy Harjo, "Skeleton of Winter,"
 from *She Had Some Horses,*
 Thunders Mouth Press, New York/
 Chicago, 1983, p. 31.

Foreword

Lucy R. Lippard

This book tells about five artists trying to lose themselves in time, or about five artists finding themselves in place. They have followed a trail of mysterious images to distant, isolated places that can seem timeless, or at least of another time. Rock art in the United States goes back at least to 1000 B.C. Its neglect by archeologists (frustrated by precisely the elusiveness that attracts the artists) has left it a nearly open field. Sheltered in caves or under vast cliffs, or starkly and subtly etched on single boulders, or perched on inaccessible heights, these images of humankind, animals, and nature were inscribed, pecked, painted, and drawn by peoples vanquished by the putative ancestors of the artists who now respond to them with such whole hearts.

This project, then, may be a kind of exorcism. The victors' heirs return to the sites because in some ways the voices of the vanquished are more eloquent than the voices that eclipsed them. In the awesome spaces of mountain and desert, on the neglected peripheries of urban centers, lost under artificial lakes, the glyphic figures of rock art are often more "live" than the falsely animated faces on television—far-seeing too.

It is a long distance between the concerns of indigenous peoples living in a huge, unboundaried continent, and the concerns of contemporary artists confined by a market foreign to art, looking to greater and lesser degrees to escape into other times, or to places that seem foreign to these times. Art for art's sake all too often denies, is even threatened by, the hybrid sources underlying virtually everything, that part of the identity of anything that is always shifting and remating, the "other" entering from other cultures. Photography is the dominant means of "pinning something down." So maybe photography of such ancient sites contradicts their essence, which is transformation. But on another level, the photographers parallel the original longing for communication that defines art at its most fundamental; they do this by attempting the impossible, becoming surrogates for the original artists. Rick Dingus insists that the project is not an escape, but a reaffirmation of our place in the world, a potential realignment of "psychic, mythic and physical interactions with the land" so they make sense in contemporary life.

As artists, Linda Connor, Rick Dingus, Steve Fitch, John Pfahl, and Charles Roitz are performing a quasi-ritual act, a pilgrimage. Relating to the shape/form/line of the image itself, to the place, to the horizon, they come back around by introducing themselves, and the camera's "present moment" to the place and to the distant "other." They seem more involved in searching than in finding. Several of them insist that they know little about the rock art they pursue and don't *want* to get into the "intellectual stuff" on an anthropological and historical basis: "If the power's there, you'll feel it," says Roitz.

The stunning imagery of the petroglyphs provides an excuse to be looking for something none of us is going to find, or something which, once momentarily found, will escape again and can thus be sought again and again, always holding out the possibility of a renewed process, or actual and psychic journey. The glyphs can provide a frame toward which to wander, away from "civilization," but not so far as to get lost. Yet as Roitz observes, more important than the contextual framing are those essential elements that go "beyond the physical characteristics of object and place—organized intuitively in an appropriate form . . . all the things that make something what it is." He activates this concept structurally. A Peruvian relief exposed below ground is echoed by a triangle of vegetation sprouting above; a rock-drawn performer appears to be dancing to the centrifugal flash of a cactus growing beside it.

Most of the artists use the 8 × 10 camera because it allows for both detail and scope, for examination of image and simultaneously a breathing space, a sense of the surroundings. The sites, monuments in themselves, are often striking in their placement, their coincidence with geological transformation, and their hermetic cultural data. A good artist can put all this together. (Anna Sofaer discovered the Fajada Butte solar and lunar observatory in Chaco Canyon while photographing petroglyphs; it was her "artist's eye" that led her to speculate about the dagger of light approaching what might have been merely "yet another spiral.") The lines are blurred between "mere documentation" (immediately disposable information) and "scientific documentation" (linked historical information), and "art" (which at best guarantees long life in the spirit of the subject).

The project proposes an alternative to the scientific closeup (and to the damaging chalking of images to make them more publishable, as though their actual existence on the site were secondary); and to the categorization that deracinates, or in Fitch's words, "lobotomizes" symbols from their context. As Dingus puts it, "our intention was not to displace or comment on the work of scientists, but to augment their work with images that respond in an alternate manner to the same subject." The project group has in fact inserted itself into a previously nonexistent space between science and art. Like their colleagues on the political art front, they are both knowledgeable and creative. As artists they have tried to communicate the moment of personal discovery, "a way of solidifying the glimpses that usually remain below the threshold of conscious perception" (Dingus). As photographers, they have established their relationships, sometimes individually, sometimes collectively, with specific places.

Sometimes the landscape is so powerful the viewer has to search the photo's surface for the human trace, all the more haunting for its hermeticism. In a Roitz photo from the Dalles in Washington, the masklike eyes (perhaps the eye-breasts of a mother goddess) suddenly animate the rock on which they are delicately pecked; they unblinkingly claim and personify the entire place. In one of Steve Fitch's large color pictures, a green and red mask (or decapitated head) emerges dreamlike from the golden rock face. In others, one-to-two-hour exposures transform a fire into a sort of eternal glow, and the "ghosts" of people who moved through the frame during the exposure recall those who moved around far earlier fires. In a Dingus altered photograph, the faces on the Thompson Wash panel (Utah) emerge not only as phantoms of a specific people, but as phantoms of our own animistic past, lost beliefs denigrated by modernity, though persistent in superstition and desire. The scribbled graphite frame feels like the wind passing over the cliff face, and the painted faces. Dingus scratches on the photographic surface in a modern counterpart to the incisions made in the rock.

Linda Connor's dark grey prints (developed by the sun, rather than chemically) also offer metaphors for the experience of discovery, prolonging by their weight and density, the moment of "arrival." She usually concentrates on the rock, the cliff, the surface rather than the vista. Her photographs seem to merge with the cliff so that the glyphs can be seen as drawn simultaneously by a hand in the past and by the artist, camera, and sun, in collaboration, today. Connor describes her first profound experience with a rock art site (a small canyon near Prescott, Arizona): "The canyon surrounded me while I felt it inside. It had no boundaries or limits, yet it was intimate. It continued to hold an occupation, the presence that had touched and marked it, yet I was alone there in the open silence. Time was lost. . . . This place and its marks did not form a 'history,' but resonated with eternity as alive as an echo."

Fitch, who is obsessed with the handprints in rock art—the most palpable outreach from one culture to another—sees rock art as a "metaphor of connectedness." This "first environmental art" has resisted the fate of the "collectable" and remained where it belongs, "integrally enclosed within a number of contexts, like something placed at the center of an expanding series of concentric circles" (to use one of the petroglyphs' most recurrent images). As "sites melt into places," these networks from the real armatures for the images, as opposed to the imposed categories and quaint or descriptive names imposed by Western scholarship, which Fitch perceives as interfering with, or "jamming" the contact between artist and place.

Roland Barthes sees effective landscape photography as that which makes a place "habitable," not "visitable." He compares it to Freud's maternal body ("there is no other place of which one can say with so much certainty that one has already been there"). Yet in this rootless society, a home is permanently out of reach for many people, and perhaps for artists in particular. Why, then, not borrow the homes of others, of the unknown? One Dingus photograph portrays an ithyphallic male triumphantly being born, or reborn, from a womb-shaped crevasse that is clearly such a powerful place that art cannot coopt it.

Perhaps the wilderness is only visitable and the photographs provide the habitation. Jerome Rothenberg has defined the wilderness as "where we don't live habitually and where we do 'return' deliberately. We have forgotten it, we say, and have to learn again to live with it. It is what survives apart from those of us who live, habitually, outside of it . . . a living world, that part of it in which the human doesn't dominate." (Wildness and bewilderment, he notes, are cognates of wilderness; and wold, or woodland, was Middle English for madness—"mind wildness.")

Rothenberg also points out that like us, indigenous people made a separation between nature and culture, or raw and cooked, though less harshly, in a less self-conscious manner: This fundamental human consciousness of being human "unites Indian and anthropologist in a common separation from—and not so common aspiration to return to—*wildness.*" (When the separation widens to an abyss, the result is a cosmic despair, reflected, I believe, in much alienated contemporary art.) It is a pity that no Native American photographer was brought into the project. The sense of location and dislocation would certainly be different from that of the white photographers. Rothenberg observes that for Acoma Pueblo poet Simon Ortiz, the "new wilderness" is "the desert of Los Angeles, the threat of human loss without the voices of the older gods, drowned out by lifeless power." In a Fitch photo, a Kachina petroglyph stands guard at the edge of Albuquerque; the city's lights flash near, or far.

The photographs provide points of reference for the wandering body, the wandering eye. Artists with a need to "get out," countered by a Western fear of aimlessness, can fuse process and product by hiking, adventuring, and "taking" a picture. There is, however, always the lurking danger of a recapitulated colonialism. One of the major concerns of the project was the recontextualization of the petroglyphs. Perhaps it is a sensitivity to cultural imperialism, rather than formalism, that has encouraged these five artists to avoid interpretation— a certain delicacy in regard to the imposition of Western identity on those we perceive as unlike ourselves. Certainly the artists generally acknowledge the myths, the shamanistic activities that are known to have existed, even though their meanings are unknown. But by "not wanting to know" about symbols, they also decontextualize the images. Integration of anthropological and artistic data seems crucial.

Similarly, however deep and whole the photographers' experience of each site, most of the artists chose to disconnect their work from their experience, to offer fragments rather than any continuous journey in space and time. Connor's work ranges from Hawaii to Texas, Roitz's from British Columbia to Peru. This intentional fragmentation is tantalizing for the viewers. Despite the loving attention paid to context— to long views and immediate textures—we are offered slipping glimpses of each site, glimpses which contradictorily focus on static, single images: one glyph, one place—even as a shadowed, hinted-at continuity lurks somewhere in the image.

In Pfahl's case, the fragmentation and hermeticism are deliberate, the core of his conceptual case. His deadpan, postcard-like color photographs of ordinary bodies of water reflect precisely that technological insensitivity that also permits the U.S. Army to buy up 100,000 acres of archaeological sites in southern Colorado and to run tanks over them. Art in our society is nice, but inconsequential. History is interesting only if it belongs to us. A Native American was asked how he felt about all the rock drawings now drowned by damming and "progress." He replied: "They're safer there."

All quotations from the artists were taken from drafts of their statements for this book, or from conversation. The Roland Barthes quotation is in Camera Lucida *(Hill and Wang, New York, 1981), p. 40. Jerome Rothenberg's "Indians and Wilderness" was published in* New Wilderness Letter *vol. 2, no. 7, Summer 1979, p. 12–16. Two other books I have found particularly useful are Polly Schaafsma's thorough* Indian Rock Art of the Southwest *(School of American Research/University of New Mexico Press, Santa Fe/Albuquerque, 1980) and the introductory* Suns and Serpents: The Symbolism of Indian Rock Art *by Gar and Maggy Packard (Packard Publications, Santa Fe, 1974).*

Rock Art: Ideas in Time and Space

Polly Schaafsma

Lower edges of towering sandstone cliffs, blue black basalt boulders resting on talus slopes exposed daily to the baking heat of the sun, eroded igneous outcrops, and lichen-covered granite in the green shade of deep woods—enigmatic designs are engraved on rocks such as these throughout the American West. Likewise the pale protected surfaces of hidden recesses of rock shelters and shallow caves display paintings made with earth pigments in various shades of red, yellow, white, black, and more rarely, green or blue. Throughout varied landscapes, rock art represents several thousand years of graphic expression by North American Indians. Paintings on stone and petroglyphs pecked, scratched, or abraded into natural rock surfaces have the distinction of being art forms that have remained through the centuries in their original settings and in which settings they had certain specific functions. Even though meanings and the symbolic import of the many motifs may be lost to the modern viewer, the mere presence of imagery within the natural scene inevitably conveys a sense of significance and heightens the sense of place.

The oldest rock art in North America was made by small bands of hunter-gatherers who occupied the continent for several thousand years. After around A.D. 1 in many parts of what is now the United States, hunter-gatherer populations were followed by horticulturalists with more complex societies who lived in sedentary villages, grew corn, beans, and squash, and who also produced rock art. Constantly changing, rock art has continued to be made by American Indians in the historic period and into the twentieth century.

Analysis of the formal attributes of imagery and of its contents has led to the identification of distinct patterns or styles which are useful to the archaeologist. These styles belong to discrete cultures and time periods and are bounded by areal limitations. The content of rock art is not random. Within any given style it consists of a limited number of elements selected from an infinite number of potential subjects. The elements chosen by rock art artists are representative of their interests, concepts, and values, which are dictated by their cultural affiliations. This is true whether the motivation for making the art was religious and part of ritual practice or whether it was secular and casual.

Both abstract and natural subjects may have symbolic value to the artist. Animals in rock art are often visual metaphorical statements of basic principles operative in the phenomenal world. These associations are usually reinforced by myth. Among the Pueblos, for example, the widely traveled duck is regarded as a searcher, messenger, and the most knowing of all creatures. Gods assume duck form in myths, and spiritual flight is accomplished in duck form. Similarly, the eagle is associated with the powers of the sun, sky, and clouds. His opposite is the turkey, a bird with limited flying ability who inhabits mountain woodlands. The latter is thus ritually related to the earth, springs, streams, and rain clouds which form on the mountains. The turkey is also associated with the dead, and turkey feathers are important in offerings to the deceased. Thus when these birds are represented in Anasazi and later Pueblo rock art, we should be aware that we are not necessarily looking at representations of various ducks, eagles, and *meleagris gallopavo* (turkeys) depicted by some prehistoric naturalist, but that these and other living creatures are often symbols which embrace a complex of powers and meanings important in Pueblo ritual and in the Pueblo description of the world. Similarly, although hunting scenes do occur, the literal interpretation that they represent game animals may be too simplistic. Mountain sheep are regarded as embodying supernatural power by virtue of their horns, and they may be symbols of fertility and prosperity. Water creatures and beast gods such as the bear and mountian lion are viewed as powerful beings by the Pueblos. Images of all of these animals in whatever form are regarded as beneficial or powerful, and we find them all in Pueblo rock art.

A clue that nature alone is not the intended subject is provided when figures combine elements that do not naturally occur together. In late Pueblo rock art mountain lions are sometimes shown wearing feathers and pointed caps. The earlier Anasazi depicted flute-playing sheep. Horned and feathered snakes in Pueblo art represent the Water Serpent, which embodies the opposing or paradoxical powers of both sky and earth, chaos and order. In some cases, important features may be exaggerated. Badgers, for example, are shown with enlarged front paws to indicate that this animal is a Medicine Society patron, valued because of his digging power which enables him to retrieve healing roots.

Abstract designs such as spirals, concentric circles, diamonds, and wavy lines occur in rock art throughout the world. Their intended meaning must be sought within each specific cultural context as the significance of such basic elements readily changes through time and between cultural groups. The same symbol may assume a variety of meanings. In the Pueblo world alone a spiral may stand for wind, water, or migrations. A simple cross stands for a star or roadrunner tracks among historic Pueblo people, or it may represent a crossing of trails (Salish) or lodges (Ojibwa). Universal meanings are indeed rare, if they exist at all.

Often in rock art one finds ambiguity in what is being represented. Ambiguity is sometimes intentional, being reserved for the most sacred and enigmatic subjects. Simple tapering human forms lacking arms and legs, for example, can be found in the unrelated work of Utah hunter-gatherers and Algonkians in southern Canada. In both cases this means of abstraction is used to signify supernaturals or shamans, or perhaps supernaturals visible only to shamans, and by no means do they represent ordinary men.[1] Abstraction contributes to the esoteric nature and power of a figure, increasing its potential for different layers of meanings. Likewise "geometric" or seemingly nonrepresentational elements may stand for a cluster of interrelated concepts.

One can conclude that imagery in rock art as well as in other media was and is important for expressing ideas and beliefs. Communication of shared ideologies is a major function of art in preliterate societies. Through the meaning of imagery cultural ties and values are stated and strengthened.

The ability of archaeologists to interpret rock art varies depending on the age of the art and whether or not living traditions of art and mythology exist that can shed light on older but historically related imagery. Something about the function of rock art can also be learned by examining its place within the landscape and how it is situated in

---

[1]For an in-depth discussion of symbol, meaning, and the iconography of space, see *Sacred Art of the Algonkians: A Study of the Peterborough Petroglyphs* by Joan M. and Romas K. Vastokas (Peterborough, Canada: Mansard Press, 1973).

relationship to other cultural remains. How is the rock art located in relationshp to specific geographic features? Does the space it occupies have potential iconographic significance? How does it relate spatially to campsites, villages, and other activity areas?

When religion was abstracted and removed from its geographic place of origin and housed in man's architectural creations, the landscape became secularized, a resource available for exploitation merely, "a land of many uses." It was no longer necessary to pray to the various resident spiritual entities or to leave offerings at appropiate places and intervals in exchange for gifts. Prior to this revolution in man's relationship with the earth, the landscape, and more specifically particular locations and outstanding features within a geographic setting, were regarded as sacred. These spots were a source or point of access to supernatural powers, and they often took on symbolic and special spiritual meaning. This type of relationship between man and landscape is still prevalent among many tribal peoples who have not given up native beliefs for participation in world religious systems. Sacred geography is the collective or tribal description of the landscape as it relates to origin and other myths which formed the background and rationale for group identity and ritual practices. The presence of rock art within the sacred landscape is not random but is often integrally related to the particular places in which it is found. Rock art may be present at springs or near distinctive rock formations where significant mythic events are said to have occurred and which are commemorated in rituals. The attribution of events to actual localities within the landscape which may be identified and visited reinforces the validity of myth. Imagery at these locations strengthens the connection between society members and their sacred past. It serves to maintain the identification of sacred locations, as well as to honor the appropriate supernaturals. It may also serve the secondary function of maintaining the definition of tribal territories and even boundaries, as certain shrines may be "owned" by particular social groups.

At shrines communication with supernaturals may take place and ritual may be enacted. Rock art not only contributes to the sacred ambiance of the location but the actual making of images may have had a ritual function. Hand prints stamped in paint at places identified as sacred may have been left in order to identify the bearer of a prayer request, or they may be left as a means of obtaining some of the power residing at the spot. Whether or not they are connected with mythic events, springs are regarded as shrines and are powerful in their own right. In the vicinity of Zuni all springs that are visited ritually during the ceremonial year are named. They are viewed as houses of the rainmakers, and inside the springs are thought to exist rain-filled inner rooms. Throughout the Pueblo Southwest prayer sticks are deposited at springs, and rock art may be associated with them as well. Open high places such as mesa tops, hills, and ridges are sometimes ascribed special significance and may bear rock art imagery, especially in the form of petroglyphs. The Pueblos sometimes built small rock enclosures to mark these sites.

The presence of rock art alone can suggest that a location is powerful. Relative newcomers to the Southwest in the sixteenth century, the Apaches and Navajo considered as sacred caves painted with imagery prior to their arrival and in turn made their own rock art in these same spots. Many eighteenth-century Navjao paintings and petroglyphs are made over earlier Pueblo figures, sometimes even incorporating them. The possibility that one is dealing with a power spot or shrine area is suggested where figures are superimposed in one place, while nearby seemingly usable surfaces remain untouched. The making of images in a specific spot seems to have been more important than the ultimate clarity of the figures, although at some Navajo sites, older paintings were actually rubbed out before new ones were made in the same place.

Shrine areas and important locations within the sacred geography may be known to most society members, in addition to the ritualists whose job it was to perform the appropriate ceremonies at these locations and who may even have been responsible for the rock art. Other rock art sites originated from more personal motives such as paintings made during a vision quest by shamans or others desiring the acquisition of power. Archeologically, these sites are indicated by their hidden locations to which access may be difficult and by their situation away from any living areas. This type of site has been described from the Chumash area of California and on the Great Plains. These locations are often considered dangerous and powerful, and the rock art at vision quest sites may be influenced by drug-induced visions and be less conventional in its symbolism. The actual act of painting at these sites was very likely accompanied by the appropriate prayers and offerings.

Other ritually directed rock art was made in connection with pragmatic functions. This includes rock art made as part of hunting and fishing ritual. Some scholars contend that many Great Basin petroglyph sites occur along prehistoric game trails at locations suitable for ambush and that the figures were made to ensure a successful hunt. Because the petroglyphs face the trails and passing game, it has been suggested that the figures themselves were thought to have power over the animals. Fertility imagery at these same sites may have been made by hunt shamans as part of a ritual request for replenishment. Similarly, in the Northwest, petroglyphs facing the ocean at the mouths of rivers are thought to have been made in these locations for the purpose of requesting supernatural aid to lure the salmon.

Recently it has been observed that certain rock art elements such as some spirals of Anasazi origin interact with beams of light in calendrically significant ways. These figures seem to have been made where shafts of sunlight hit a shadowed rock surface at times such as summer solstice, the equinoxes, or possibly on dates which anticipated ceremonial events scheduled during the solar year. Some of these sites could have functioned as sun shrines. The maintenance of a solar calendar was (and still is) particularly important for southwestern horiculturalists, whose ceremonial cycle is integrally related to the planting, growing, and harvesting of crops, events which articulate with the spiritual universe.

In contrast with sites connected with esoteric or ritual proceedings in locations apart from living areas or the daily round of activities, much rock art was made in public locations where it was seen regularly. Some of this imagery was made for specific purposes. At Hopi, boulders with petroglyphs designate various clans' ownership of fields and their boundaries. Likewise on the Northwest Coast rock art was used in historic times to mark fishing rights and the boundaries of family hunting territories and to signify trade monopolies. Between A.D. 1250 and 1300 the cliff-dwelling Anasazi of the central San Juan drainage painted large white figures wihin the rock shelters harboring their villages. These designs were usually round and conspicuously placed. Visible for long distances, these paintings may well have been emblems of the social affiliation of the group or groups occupying the dwelling. Smaller and often very casually made figures invariably are painted, pecked, or scratched on the cliff faces adjacent to the living and work space of a cliff dwelling and may have functioned, possibly inadvertently, as territorial indicators. Similar figures occur in the vicinity of Anasazi dwelling sites in open areas wherever rocks are immediately available, and the practice of making rock art near Pueblo villages has continued until the present day. Similarly, petroglyphs are common around sheep corrals, where they were probably made by herders in their idle moments. Kachinas and masks are popular figures in these public sites, just as they are in rock art made on ritual occasions in isolated areas. Nevertheless, the function of rock art made within the realm of daily living activities differs considerably from that made in "powerful" and "dangerous" locations beyond the village.[2]

Contemporary Navajo rock art in the form of paintings, petroglyphs, and charcoal drawings is often associated with herding activities. This rock art places an emphasis on horses which are highly valued among these people as well as on other rodeo subjects such as bulls and cowboys with big hats. Historic sites on the Great Plains illustrating action scenes with men, horses, guns, tipis, and so forth were often records of personal exploits as well as commemorative of historic events. Common to modern sites of all cultural origins are allusions to love and sex, names, cattle brands, initials, and dates. The latter are the product of autobiographical and self-promotional motivations similar to those underlying much modern urban graffiti.

Cultural beliefs and values are manifested in the imagery of rock art both sacred and mundane from all periods of time. With the brief exception of rock art made in the recent historic past, which is heavily influenced in subject and intent by Western concepts and their associated values, rock art is a graphic statement about a world different from our own. It originates in a different set of philosophies and different descriptions of the world—a world not organized according to scientific rules but one in which man is a part of an embracing spiritual web of relationships defined along the lines of symbolic values and metaphor. Rock art and its very presence in the landscape is a document of the relationships that existed, and in some cases continue to exist, between the various native peoples of this continent and the universe they perceive(d).

---

[2]For an excellent discussion on contemporary Zunis perception of rock art, see "Images of Power and the Power of Images: The Significance of Rock Art for Contemporary Zunis," by M. Jane Young, *Journal of American Folklore* 99, no. 387 (1985): 3–48.

I have suggested ways in which rock art can be interpreted and how some of it functioned. Yet there remain a great many rock art sites whose content is no longer interpretable and for which no reason for their particular location is now apparent. Nevertheless, for those of us who wander by in the twentieth century from other cultural backgrounds, these images communicate something of the importance or power these locations had for earlier people. Faded paintings, eroded petroglyphs, figures obscured by centuries of weathering and darkened by patina are sometimes rendered more mysterious by their evasiveness and lack of explicit meaning. The photographs and photo-drawings in this book are a contemporary statement about an ongoing response to rock art and its context—the landscapes and immediate setting in which it is found.

Gestures of Faith

Linda Connor

Growing up in New England I had no idea what a petroglyph was, but chance eventually brought me to a site on Highway 50 in Nevada, then to another in Dinosaur National Monument. Later my aunt and uncle took me to the mysterious inscribed boulder in the jungle of St. Vincent Island. By then I had become curious. I wanted to see more.

It was not until 1976, however, that I really experienced one of these places, a small canyon with petroglyphs near Prescott, Arizona, where I spent a few quiet hours photographing. The winter sun was radiant, the quartz veins and mica shone, and the silence had a warm weight. The spirals and marks were weathered and seemed as much a part of that canyon as the stars in the night sky. That afternoon a magic entered me, slowly and delicately like the tiny bubbles materializing and rising to the surface of water put on to boil. It is in my blood now, recurring sometimes spontaneously, at other times only after I consciously slow down enough to respond to the place and its marks.

That small canyon gave me a new understanding of place. It brought perceptions that I had often thought of as disparate into a new whole. The canyon surrounded me, while I felt it internally. My usual sensation of being separate within an environment dissolved. I felt both the presence of those who had made the marks and the independent vibrancy of the drawings. Their animated power joined me in the open silence. Time seemed lost—not just my few hours of absorption, but human time, cultural time, geologic time. This place and its marks were not enclosed in a history; they resonated with eternity as alive as an echo.

For the past ten years I have photographed and visited rock art sites whenever and wherever I could. Friends and park rangers give me directions and then ask if I know the ones in such and such a canyon? Most of the sites come to me this way, by word of mouth, as shared

1. Petroglyphs, near Prescott, Arizona.

2. Thom and Susan looking at petroglyphs, Puget Sound, Washington, 1983.

discoveries often shrouded with a layer of protectiveness. Because of the location of most rock art, sites searching and scrambling are often necessary, though the recent acquisition of a pair of binoculars has been most helpful. I love the quest, in spite of the feeling of being lost, my anxiety about some dirt roads, and the difficulty of following someone else's directions in unfamiliar terrain. Why is it there always seems to be a barrier of "cat's claw" bushes exactly where I want to place my tripod? But I find a satisfaction in learning where to look for the markings, on which type of rock and surface, and I usually agree with the maker that the site was well chosen. The glyphs are invariably in special places, a canyon with water, a cave, a prominent rock or ledge that affords the best view.

The searching out of these sites has proved an advantage for much of my other work, though indirectly. Often the hardest part of photography is getting out the door. Motivation and a plan are needed. I use the impetus of a search for rock art to carry me along while reminding myself to keep my eyes open for other things. If I fail to locate the rock art site, or if it defies my efforts to photograph it well (impossible location, high winds, difficult light, to say nothing of human error), I work on other images along the way. It is a good arrangement.

I once spent most of a day at Puget Sound getting directions to a large beach boulder with petroglyphs, then walking miles with my friends Thom and Susan only to find the tide in and the stone half submerged in the sea. The glyphs were facing the water and very faint with age. The site did not want to be photographed, but I saw Thom and Susan looking at the carvings and made a photograph of them. Another time on Quadra Island, British Columbia, the petroglyphs on the beach stones were so worn that the only clear image I made was one of the two young brothers holding their rubbing.

It is useful to have a purpose, a focus of attention, but not at the

3. Brothers holding a rubbing, Quadra Island, British Colombia, Canada, 1981.

exclusion of seeing other things. Once in Canyon de Chelly, after intently photographing the petroglyphs on a wide ledge, I turned around and "saw" for the first time the landscape and space that had faced them for 800 years.

When other tourists see me working with my 8 × 10 their first question is about the camera; next they invariably ask, "What do the Indian writings mean?" They are disappointed to learn that I know little more than they do, assuming that anyone who would fuss with such equipment must be an expert. I am comfortable with not knowing. Often just the petroglyphs' placement, the energy of the drawing, and the relationship they hold with their environment are enough for me. The reward is delight, not information.

My conviction has grown that the drawings served a complex range of purposes for the people who made them, from casual to the most intense spiritual expression. There are the panels of Shamanistic visions (Plate 2), the intimate handprints of a family on the cliff wall behind a crumbling adobe, the recently rediscovered solstice markers used to reaffirm a community calendar (Plate 9). Though most of the marks remain mute and mysterious, they are clearly infused with meaning. Their presence announces an intention to signify and communicate even though we are not privy to their message.

The photographs made on my trip to Asia share a similarity with the rock art work in this regard. These images confront us with information and symbols that defy our Western rationality. I am intrigued by their capacity to give a glimpse of another world view and another manner of expression.

The nonspecificity of rock art allows me to overlay my shading and personal meaning. I do not want to reinterpret the symbols, but I do find that their open meaning allows me an access that would be denied if they were not muted by time and dislocated from their cultural matrix. An interesting exception is the photograph of the Spanish alphabet at Inscription Rock, New Mexico (Plate 13), which in context with the other rock art images suggests a dialogue between "primitive" and "modern" civilizations. Although made like the petroglyphs, this inscription presents a map of language rather than the Anasazi's world of symbols.

I usually avoid photographing sites with current cultural artifacts, fencing, graffitti, tourist trash, and park service signs. At times though, I will photograph out of anger and despair at what is happening to so many of these ancient places, through vandalism or the insensitivity of the powers that profess to protect them. As the shot gun scars and graffiti attest, our culture often does not coexist gracefully with the remains of this earlier indigenous culture. Has this always been the case? Figure 6 shows an image from northern India of Buddhist symbols placed defiantly on the earlier petroglyphs of a hunter-gatherer culture, announcing a new order. Two of the world's most densely drawn rock art sites, in eastern California, lie within the boundaries of a naval missile testing range. On the wall of Little Petroglyph Canyon I found a neatly pecked $E = MC^2$. Once while photographing at Three Rivers, New Mexico (Plate 16), I could not shake the ominous realization that those stones and markings stood witness to the first atomic bomb explosion at White Sands, which lies only a few miles away.

Although I am distressed by these cultural dissonances, this is not

10 *Gestures of Faith*

4. (upper left) Petroglyphs, Hawaii, 1978.
5. (lower left) Petroglyphs, Hawaii, with Park Service ramp, 1983.
6. (above) Petroglyphs superinscribed with Buddhist Chörtens, Ladakh, India, 1985.

what my work is about. Nor is it about a particular temporal and local context, such as the late twentieth-century western landscape. Photography most often is used and read within a specific context and it can articulate beautifully what we collectively consider to be reality. But the tables can be turned. My aim is to photograph in a way that denies time and our social context by avoiding the cultural clues and choosing subjects and symbols that extend through time and societies. Progress and history interest me less than the eloquence of human imagination as it flows from all time, the paleolithic to the present.

The petroglyphs display an essence of ritual meaning and spirit. For me the rose windows at Chartres are no greater a manifestation of spirit than the figures of the Great Gallery. I love knowing that the cathedral at Chartres, the "erotic" temples of Kharjaraho, India, and many of the finest rock art panels in the Southwest were all made during the twelfth

Linda Connor

century. They are all infused with a spirit which is still apparent and resonating today. When I photograph I try to organize the image to best describe this shape of spirit. Sometime I will do this by using symmetry or by collapsing space and scale. At other times I will use certain qualities of light or the surroundings to intensify the presence of the mark.

The longer I work the more essential it becomes that my photographs honor what they represent. I am continually challenged to produce photographs that are truthful to the petroglyphs and that also serve my expression. I achieve the balance by photographing the subject in a clear and unmannered way while satisfying my sense of design. The photograph then joins and interacts with my other images, suggesting new ways to see and understand it. My most successful photographs look quite simple, though they usually contain multiple meanings that can

7. (upper left) Temple, Kharjaraho, India, 1979.
8. (lower left) Spiral, Nasca, Peru, 1984.
9. (below) Nighthawk with eggs, Colorado, 1982.

be drawn out by association with other images or by their sequence. For instance, when I juxtapose the image of the spiral geoglyph from Nasca, Peru, with the image "Nighthawk with Eggs," a visual colliding and blending occur that does not change the character of either image. Rather their combined resonance creates expanded meanings. In a similar way a poet will combine imagery or sounds that trigger other references into play. Images and symbols can link freely like agreeable atoms to form new substances of their parts.

    I particularly enjoy interweaving the rock art photographs with my landscapes. This seems to *place* the images of rock art while bringing a human presence to the images of the land. I feel this human presence strongly when I visit these sites.

    I've come to believe that often the drawings were done to channel and mitigate the awe one feels in response to the powers of the surrounding universe. My photography is a similar attempt, a gesture of faith. The marks and photographs form a link, however slight and human, between our mortality and the continuance beyond us.

1. Figure and Serpent, Utah, 1984.

2. Great Gallery, Horseshoe Canyon, Utah, 1982.

3. Kachina Kiva, Utah, 1982.

4. Petroglyphs and Palo Verde, Picacho Mountains, Arizona, 1985.

5. Petroglyphs, Sears Point, Arizona, 1985.

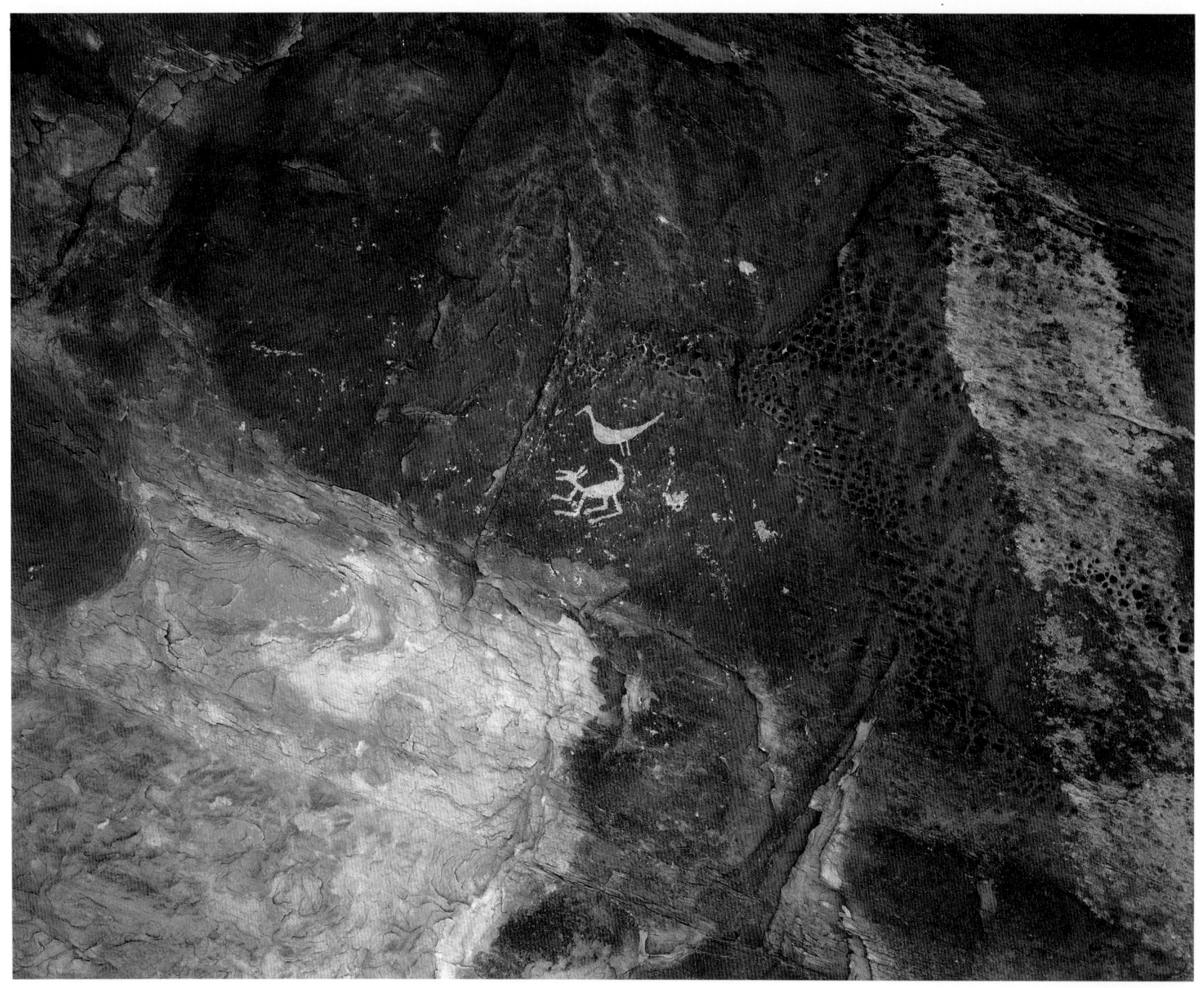

6. Coyote and Bird, Arizona, 1981.

7. Petroglyph, Hawaii, 1983.

8. Spanish Entering Canyon de Chelly, Arizona, 1982.

9. Solstice, Hovenweep, Utah, 1984.

10. Petroglyphs, Utah, 1982.

11. Double Spiral, Zuni, New Mexico, 1985.

12. Zigzag, Zuni, New Mexico, 1986.

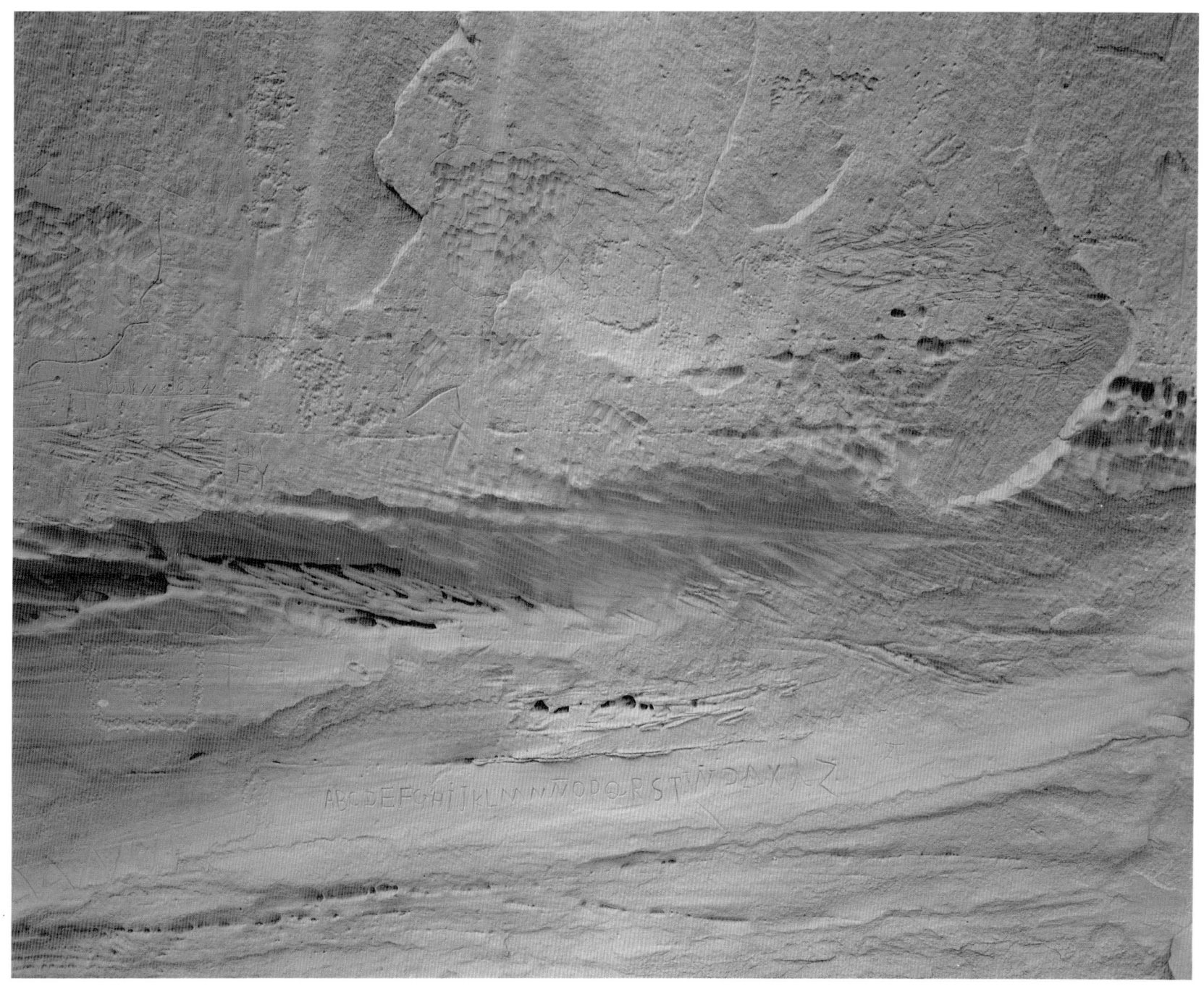

13. Spanish Alphabet, Inscription Rock, New Mexico, 1983.

14. Animal-Shaped Rock, near Bishop, California, 1982.

15. Animal-Shaped Rock, near Bishop, California, 1981.

16. Bighorn Sheep, Three Rivers, New Mexico, 1982.

17. Comet Panel, Arizona, 1986.

18. Petroglyph Rock, Toro Muerto, Peru, 1984.

19. Spirit Figures, Great Gallery, Horseshoe Canyon, Utah, 1984.

20. Hands, Canyon de Chelly, Arizona, 1982.

Places, Dreams, and Journeys: Long-Term Contexts for Now and Later

Rick Dingus

The photographs in this project are personal; they acknowledge that we were participants in a process of making new images about old locations and the marks they contain. Our intention was not to displace or comment on the work of scientists who have also studied American Indian rock art sites but to augment their work with images that respond in an alternate manner to the same subject. Instead of applying a single methodology in our study, each of us was free to respond in whatever manner seemed appropriate. In fact, many of us happened to photograph some of the same places but from very different viewpoints.

Perhaps most important of all, the rock art is not the only subject of this project, but the main object of our attention, which we used to enlarge our awareness of the present moment. By including the here and now in our pictures we emphasize that, like the rock art itself, our photographs are also artifacts; they record contemporary sensibilities responding to the same places that once were important to other people. Throughout the project we attempted to discover a continuity that links the past with the present and future. Each journey to a site was like a pilgrimage to a special place, full of new understandings and new awarenesses. By sharing our photographs we hope to do more than simply share our experience—we hope to invite others to participate in the dialogue and generate new viewpoints of their own.

Since the images we created were as much personal as they were collective, the work that each of us did related to what we had done before. Long before I began to photograph rock art sites for this project, I kept stumbling onto them inadvertently. Interested in the land as visible evidence of natural forces at work over immense spans of geologic time, I was surprised to find that places which physically manifested geological transformations were sometimes the same places that contained rock art.

After photographing features in the landscape and discovering petroglyphs or pictographs, I soon began to photograph them, too, in relation to their surroundings.

The photography I did for the Rephotographic Survey Project (RSP) also related to what I did here. In the RSP we retraced the steps of nineteenth-century expeditionary photographers through the American West and made repeat photographs of the same sites today. We tested the tolerances of photographic documentation as an objective tool to measure, study, and compare changes at sites after a hundred years had passed.

Like the RSP, the rock art project offered the opportunity to explore similar ideas, but in different ways. It was a chance to step back in time much further than one hundred years and to visit places that people have interacted with for many hundreds and, in some cases, thousands of years. But, instead of sites that were important to nineteenth-century American explorers, this time we photographed places that were important to indigenous people.

By choosing to interact in a more personal way while photographing the rock art, it wasn't my intention to abandon objectivity but to acknowledge its relativity and to juxtapose it with other aspects equally important. In the photo-drawings that make up my work here, the photographic information is still tied to objective features of the world, but my hand-drawn marks are a spontaneous and gestural counterpoint to the precise, analytical clarity of the camera's recording of external detail. In some ways these marks represent pure energy—lines of force, natural process, and the invisible transforming movements of time. Yet they are also an overlay, the aim of which is to further an awareness of more than the immediate surroundings or what current attitudes about time and place habitually condition us to see. They help solidify the glimpses that usually remain below the threshold of conscious perception.

The mythical implications of the things I photograph are as important as their implications in terms of natural or historical facts. Likewise, the act of making photographs is tied to waking, rational reality, but the act of drawing is meditative and dreamlike. Combining the two is like synthesizing and restoring balance to the two sides of existence that many suppose are opposites, but for me they are equal parts of the same continuum, as night completes day. The photo-drawings are like magical fetishes that are as much the product of inner states as they are of external circumstances. They are part of an ongoing event—a gesture of participation with change on a psychic as well as a physical level, a means of interacting with places, people, and the forces that continue to create and reform the world we live in.

The rock art has been an important catalyst for these interactions. In my memory it shifts and changes, as do the places that contain it. I'm astounded at how different the sites appear when I return to them after a period of time. I can never tell how much the changes are inside of me and how much they are in the places themselves—in the light, season, and weather, in the impact of other visitors.

There is a cave in northern New Mexico that I revisit whenever I happen to be in the vicinity. Each return extends my relationship with the place, reaffirming past interactions while also providing new and important experiences. From the outside it is but a small and dark vertical slit, surrounded by similar openings, on a light-colored cliff of volcanic rock (Plates 21 and 22). A few steps have been carved to aid one's entrance up and into the cave; the opening is just large enough to crawl through. Inside is a small chamber, squared at the bottom, rounded overhead. The surfaces of the ceiling and walls have been blackened with smoke and charcoal, contrasting with the deeply carved light-colored petroglyphs of animals and anthropomorphic figures which circle the interior.

Nowhere else have I seen rock art that exemplifies such an integrated handling of a complete environment, from the subtle alteration of the physical space to the careful interaction, spacing, and animated gesture of each carved form. The depicted battles, transformations, and dancing movements all come alive with intense feeling as one sits inside the cave. Though the interior is small and intimate, it feels expansive, almost infinite, as if the black walls were disappearing into a night sky, the stark figures looking like distant constellations of stars. Outside it may be daytime, but inside this cave it always feels like night, submerged in the deep, dark pool of a powerful dream.

Features of the cave invite interpretation. The entrance itself resembles a female vulva; the x-ray skeletal motif and transformation of anthropomorphic figures into hybrid half-human beings inside all point to shamanism and the symbolism of death and spiritual rebirth within the womb of the earth mother. But given the displacements in time and culture, we will probably never know the actual meaning these features had for those who created them.

Regardless of the fact that the place may forever defy our attempts to explain it, the first time I entered was like passing a threshold. By simply being there I knew something which changed my preconceptions about the past. There was also something vital and relevant to contemporary life about these images and this place. In spite of the fact that it was strange and new to me, it was also surprisingly familiar. The depicted events and the place itself recalled my dreams of similar events and places and reminded me that, in the subconscious at least, some aspects of our relationship to the natural world have not changed much throughout the centuries.

Memories are like dreams in that each time we relive them they change and shift with our changing attitudes toward the things we remember. Associations from past experiences also help orient our new experiences. Impressed by the unique qualities of places I've been and the unspoken secrets contained in rock art, my dreams reflect back old associations while creating new ones. Like vivid memories, the important dreams never fade but color my other recollections and partially condition my new experiences of actual rock art.

One dream I had about rock art is worth recounting here. It has influenced my interactions with sites ever since:

> I was hiking in the desert with my wife on a cool and crisp day in late winter. The stillness and quiet were like a vacuum; a tingling and vibrant edge of clarity surrounded everything. The earth stretched out to the horizon—warm, comforting, and beautiful to see.
>
> I was standing within the spiraling vortex of a monumental arch of sandstone, bordered by towering slabs of rock on either side. We had paused as we climbed through this magnificent window to look at an unusual formation off in the distance. It was a stone pinnacle that was somehow special, reminding me of the lofty perches of a Greek monastery.
>
> Then I noticed a small panel of petroglyphs carved near its base. Suddenly there was a loud roll of thunder. The ground beneath our feet began to shake; small stones and debris went tumbling and sliding down the slope. It seemed as if the land was about to split wide open and swallow us whole. Yet while all of this happened we were dumbstruck and glued to the spot because of what we were seeing. At the first crack of thunder, the petroglyphs had zoomed forward to fill completely our field of vision. Slowly they began to move and change; soon they assumed many forms in rapid succession and became almost a blur of images superimposed over each other. They changed so fast I can't remember what we saw, except that each image was clear and complete, in continuous motion, and tied to all of the rest. It seemed that all of eternity was passing before our eyes in a few brief moments.
>
> Abruptly, the images began to fade, and we remembered our fear. But just as we were about to run, the rumbling ceased and the ground stopped shaking. In place of the distant rock column an object was beginning to form. A large vessel, like an Anasazi pot, a Greek amphora vase, or a Chinese ritual urn, slowly appeared. On its outer surface was the rock art once more—stick figures moving and gesturing for a few instants only. And then, as suddenly as this all had begun, it silently vanished. The strange column of rock was back in its place, and the desert was again still and quiet as if nothing unusual had happened.

Not long after the dream, I was traveling through west Texas searching for a rock art site. After miles and miles of wrong turns on dirt roads in a deserted area near the Mexican border, a friend and I finally located a painted cave I had been to years before (Plate 32). I stepped inside to make a photograph with my electronic strobe. Simultaneous with the flash of my camera, lightning struck outside the cave and a summer cloudburst was upon us. The lightning flashed again and again, startling us with each booming thunderclap, the ground shaking as each shock wave passed through us, reverberating through our chests like the beat of a drum. Rain began dripping from the entrance of the shallow cave into a catch basin the Indians had carved in front of the painted form of Quetzalcoatl, the plumed serpent. Coyote, Bear, Turtle, Bird, and others were there too, painted in faded white on the low, smoke-blackened ceiling.

Storms like this are not uncommon, but the coincidence of its timing, coupled with the mythic presence of the place and the events that led us there, recalled my dream and gave added significance to an event already powerful and moving. But our enthusiasm for the storm, as for the rock art in my dream, was tempered by a nagging anxiety—this time that we would now be stuck in a remote location with impassable roads.

In an area potentially dangerous with many sorts of illegal traffic, it seemed unwise to linger here overnight.

But when the storm was over, all was revitalized and renewed. The air was clean and sweet-smelling; the cactus and other plant life glistened, in full bloom. A flash flood had destroyed one of the roads by which we attempted to return, but not the one we were supposed to be on. Any trouble we encountered, real or imagined, was more than repaid by our experience at that place.

Not many rock art sites provide experiences as dramatic as the ones just mentioned. Undoubtedly, there are many kinds of rock art that reflect various human interactions with many different environments. Each of us would probably choose different favorites, if what we liked was all that mattered.

It's easy to impose drama or become obsessed with a favorite idea and then see it reflected in whatever we happen to come across. Some rock art enthusiasts see every concentric circle or spiral petroglyph as another archeoastronomical observation point because it has been demonstrated that some sites do function that way. Others are hard-nosed pragmatists who see nothing but the clockwork mechanisms of economics and physical survival; they attribute sympathetic magic to rock art as a "primitive control" over hunted game and a frightening world.

Though there are bits of truth in each of these theories that are applicable to specific sites, they oversimplify so much that they reveal more about the inadequacy of current interpretation than anything else. Likewise we seem to have always projected our own hopes and fears onto indigenous peoples. The idea of the "noble savage" coincided with our own desire for innocence and a return to nature but came nowhere close to describing the complexity or diversity of Native American lifestyles or belief systems. Similarly, our label of "savage barbarian" came precisely at the time we were playing the role of the barbarian, invading and attempting to conquer their culture and ties to the land we wanted.

In my curiosity about contemporary American Indian attitudes, as opposed to the stereotype images we have assigned to them, my journeys to rock art have also led me to contemporary Indians. Sometimes they have accompanied me to rock art sites. Once I was taken to a sacred ruin, introduced to the "ancient spirits" that resided there with a simple ceremony, and told stories about the place that again reminded me of my dreams.

Last summer in northern Arizona I met traditional Hopi and Navajo leaders while accompanying Dan Budnik, a friend long familiar with the area and the people who live there. Invited into the Indian homes, we showed them our photographs of rock art and discussed the similarities and differences between the white world and theirs.

The Indians enjoyed looking at our photographs but usually did not have a lot to say about the rock art. Partly this was because some of our pictures were of places far enough removed in time or geography that they were not directly related to these people. Partly, they seemed to view the rock art as but one fragment from a richly woven fabric of activity, the implications of which touched on religious beliefs not commonly discussed. Mostly, it seemed that for them explanations were beside the point.

Late one day we visited a petroglyph site in the company of Katherine Smith, a respected Navajo elder from Big Mountain. Nearby the many Hopi clan symbols, she searched out a lone sun symbol and centered her attention lovingly on it. She removed her moccasins for traction and climbed half way up a slope of large tumbled boulders so she could stand respectfully, silently viewing the vast space and the sun as it passed below the horizon. Before we left, she collected samples of the red and green-colored earth from there to take home with her.

Later that week we slept one night in Katherine's hogan. That night I had another vivid dream:

> I had returned from my journey with the Indians and was at a late night party with friends. I went outside on the balcony to get some fresh air. I looked up in the sky and noticed the full moon rising. But it looked like it was moving across the sky too fast, and I was concerned that something was wrong.
>
> I went back into the party for a while and then came back outside. The moon had already crossed the sky and was now making a second pass, faster and moving closer, looking much larger than before. This time I was afraid. I thought it meant the earth was going out of orbit. I went inside and told some others but no one paid much attention.
>
> I returned for a third time to the balcony, and this time it was certain. The moon loomed ominously and so large on the

horizon that it nearly filled half of the black sky. There was a violent lurching of the ground beneath me.

I saw the earth wobbling on its axis as if it might spin completely off its course in the solar system, its magnetic poles were shifting abruptly, its whole surface was heaving beneath the pressure.

Earthquakes and volcanic eruptions on a global scale set loose a chain of destruction. All around me people were dying, and I thought this was the end for all of us. But all at once something happened. The earth righted itself and established a new orbit. Much had been lost, but now there was a settling of dust and ashes, a clearing away of the air, and a new calm after the storm.

The next day Katherine's niece and her husband, Louise and George Crittenden, took us into the back country to meet more "traditionals." At one point Louise said to me, "I hope you understand what I mean when I say these people are traditional. Being traditional doesn't mean they don't have a pick-up truck or have a TV set in their hogan. It means they have a good heart and keep the old ways alive inside as they adapt to the changing world around them."

One of the people we met was Dan Chee, a ninety-year-old Navajo Medicine Man still fit enough to ride a horse as his usual means of transportation. He was trim, alert, and energetic, with strength and clarity to his every word and movement.

As he walked out from his hogan to meet us, he gestured toward a nearby sacred peak, the kind of place where I would expect to find rock art. With a twinkle in his eye, he jokingly remarked in Navajo that the peak was "his mountain." Then he laughed at the absurdity of anyone pretending they could own it. That peak is his mythical source of power, but he seemed to be saying that, if anything, it was he who is owned by it, not the reverse.

Further discussions underlined his view of humanity's place within the context of a larger system. We asked him what was causing the Hopi-Navajo relocation problems. Instead of blaming the Hopi or Navajo tribal councils, the American government, or the big businesses that want to exploit the natural resources of the land, he described the situation as "one of the tests provided by the times we are in—the Earth is out of balance, going through a time of trouble, a cycle of change . . . and people, too, are out of balance. There will soon be many changes, major ones that will affect us all."

As this was being translated into English, his eyes held mine in direct contact with gentle strength. I felt a jolt in my stomach and hovered between trying to understand what he was saying, remembering my dream from the night before, and wondering if there was any connection between the two.

We asked if there was anything we could do to help.

"I need some dental work," he said, pointing to the four teeth he had left, three of which looked as if they needed to be pulled.

"We'll try to put you in touch with a dentist friend in Santa Fe," we said. "But is there anything we can do to help the overall situation?"

"That's easy," he replied. "Don't waste your time dwelling on past or present injustices. Pray to the Creator and show your appreciation for the natural forces he has set in motion. Understand your place within that scheme so you may endure your hardships with a sense of purpose and make a contribution. If you use the powers you have been given to use for the right purposes, if you think, act, and pray for the earth you will help it through its time of trouble."

Our search for rock art may have led us to ancient places, but the experiences it has provided have not separated us from the present world but reaffirmed our place within it. More important than any single experience is how each of us has realigned our understanding of and involvement with the ordinary affairs of daily life. The rock art has led to psychic, mythic, and physical interactions with the land; it has led to soul-searching discussions with indigenous people about the continuities and differences between the old ways and the new ways. Most important of all, it has given contemporary life a new context and expanded the sense of place everywhere to include the present as part of the same great process that goes back to the beginning.

The ongoing traditions of Native people still emphasize mythical and sacred connections to the land and the natural forces that created it and all of life. Western civilization, however, has traded the integrating capacity of myth for the discriminating illusions of objectivity. We may recognize the dictates of natural law as defined by our science, but somehow the scientific method, which was designed not to influence what we studied, has been carried over to influence how we view our relationship with the world at large.

We pretend that humanity is separate from nature, and we act as if the natural world exists only for our own use. We constantly debate political questions about culture, sex, and economics but rarely acknowledge the larger natural system that contains the human situation within it. Before we dismiss all of myth as outmoded superstition, let us beware the limitations of our own mechanistic attitudes and the dangerous temptations they have provided us with. Is it possible that, in the same way that our conscious reality is balanced and advised by the unconscious workings of our minds, our rational actions need the balancing effects of myth to keep them from their own excesses?

Instead of focusing on short-term wants, needs, and solutions in a material sense alone, let us consider as well the psychic demands for survival and the long-term effects of our actions here on earth. If we relinquish our short-sighted and anthropocentric orientation we may yet survive into the next century. For the good of us all, may we restore the balance and remember the larger pattern as we take part in its process.

21. Exterior: Cave Kiva in northern New Mexico (Rebirth Place), 1982–86.

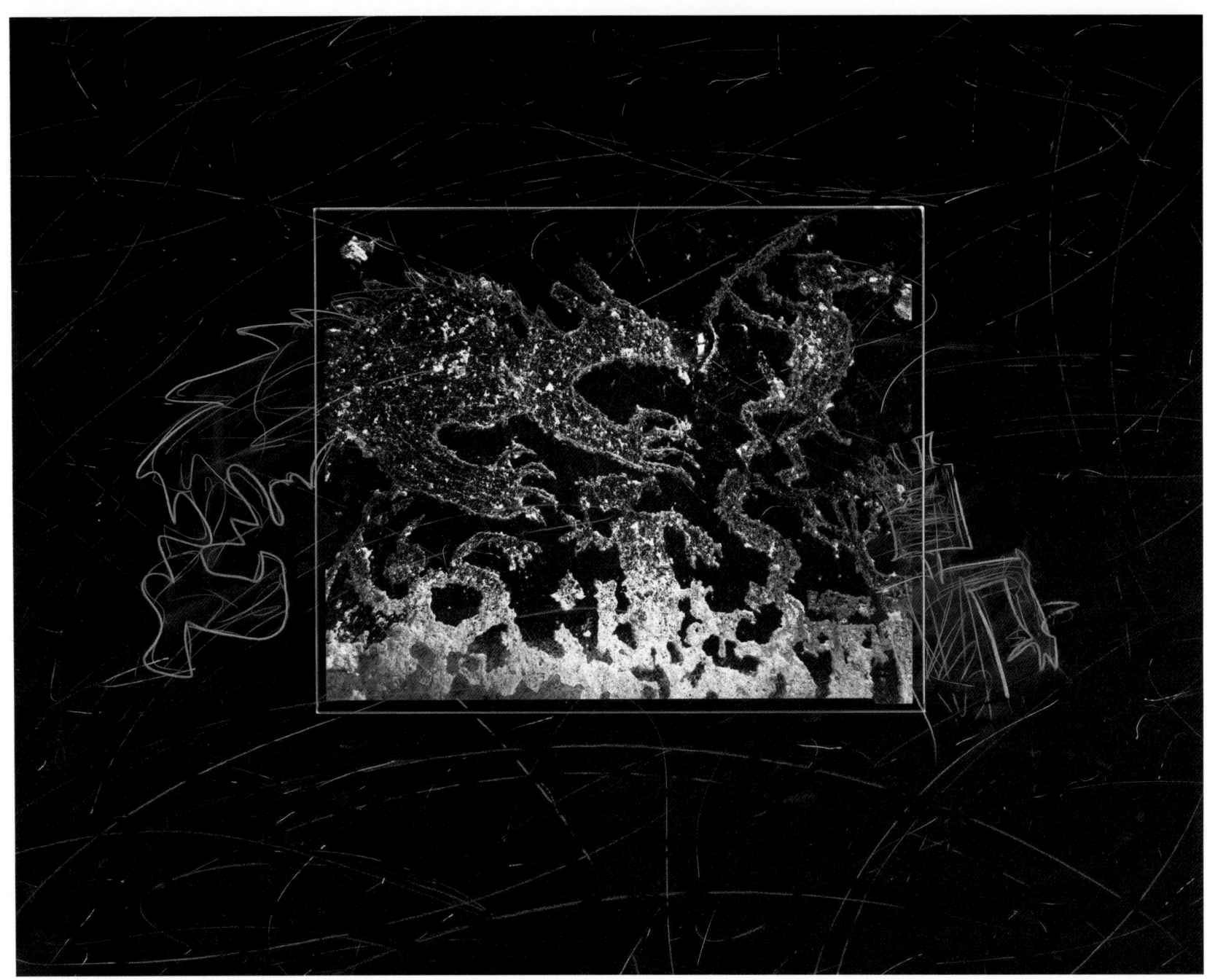

22. Interior: Cave Kiva in northern New Mexico (Mythical Fragments), 1983–85.

23. Cave Spirit, Canyonlands, Utah, 1982–84.

24. Figures Above a Ruin, Canyonlands, Utah, 1982.

25. "Thirteen Faces," Canyonlands, Utah, 1982–86.

26. Location of the "Sky Faces," Canyonlands, Utah, 1982–84.

27. "Five Portraits" Ceremonial, Davis Canyon, Utah (Proposed Nuclear Waste Disposal Site), 1982–86.

28. Displaced References, Canyonlands, Utah, 1983–86.

29. Snake Dance, Thompson Wash, Utah, 1982–86.

30. Cliff Petroglyph, northern New Mexico, 1984.

31. Catch Basin Boulder, northern New Mexico, 1985–86.

32. Plumed Serpent in a Painted Cave near Ft. Hancock, Texas (after the Storm), 1984–85.

33. Painted Rock near Santa Barbara, California, 1983–84.

34. "Tlaloc" Shelter, Hueco Tanks, Texas, 1984.

35. "Tlaloc" near Cooks Peak, New Mexico, 1984–86.

36. Repeating the Pattern, Three Rivers, New Mexico, 1983–84.

37. Marking the Passage, Three Rivers, New Mexico, 1983–86.

38. Storytelling Rocks, northern New Mexico, 1984–86.

39. Handprints in a Cave, Canyonlands, Utah, 1982–86.

40. Fitch's Fire, northern New Mexico, 1984–86.

About Being in Places

Steve Fitch

In southeastern Utah on the Colorado plateau and in a region known as the Four Corners, there is a deep and narrow canyon that runs for over fifty miles from the Abajo Mountains into the San Juan River. Besides several cliff dwellings and other Pueblo ruins are numerous rock art sites in the canyon, not only those of the Anasazi and earlier Basketmakers but also "abstract" pictographs made by older Archaic peoples. About halfway between the headwaters of the canyon and its junction with the San Juan River is one small group of pictographs that consists simply of pairs of actual hand prints, some made with red paint, others with white (Fig. 1).

 Around one hundred prints in all, they are grouped above a small ledge on the south wall of the canyon about fifty feet off the canyon floor. The red prints are grouped together on the left, while most of the white prints are clustered on the right. The positive hand prints in this group are similar to those found at hundreds, perhaps even thousands, of sites throughout the Anasazi region of the Southwest. One also finds hand prints that are negative, where the paint—usually red or white—was sprayed around a hand held to the rock surface. Less common are sites where the hand print is actually a pecked "simulation" of a real print or, perhaps rarest of all, a pecked representation of a negative, sprayed hand print such as occurs on the Comanche Gap hogback in New Mexico (Fig. 2). Probably a majority of the painted hand prints that I have seen occur at or near an Anasazi ruin. This one group of prints, however, is not located near a ruin but instead is situated by itself at a gradual bend in the canyon, and is located high up in a fairly visible location. It is nicknamed "the FBI panel."

 In 1982 I visited the site while backpacking through the canyon after a ranger at Natural Bridges National Monument had marked its location on my topographical map along with a number of other sites also located there. Whenever I come upon Anasazi or other prehistoric hand prints

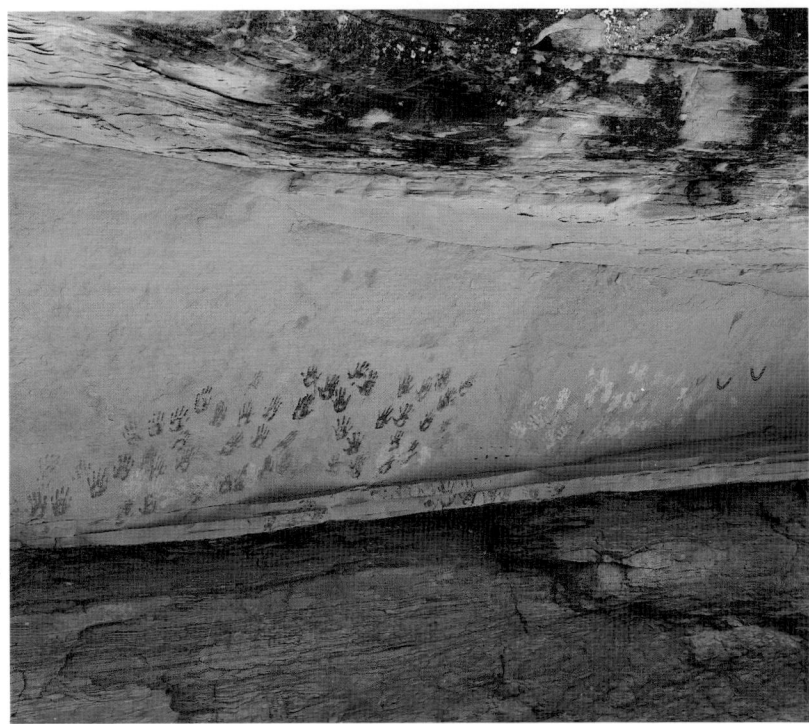

1. "The FBI Panel" in southeastern Utah, October 12, 1982.

2. Hand print, Comanche Gap.

my response is usually the same: a curious inspection of the prints themselves, a look around the place they are located in, and an inconclusive puzzling about "what they mean." At the FBI panel I puzzled over several questions. Why the two colors of paint and the two groups of prints? Were the two colors representative of two different clans or of male and female? Why were they made—as a gesture of participation in a ceremony or to designate some kind of witnessing? Were they made all at one time or over many years? And why at this place in the canyon? Was this an initiation place, a place of prayer, or a site from which to gain some kind of special power or material? Maybe the group of prints was a territorial designation, perhaps a boundary marker.

What struck me as being odd at the time was the name of the site: the FBI panel. At first it seemed merely clever or a bit funny, but it started me thinking about other prehistoric sites with a similar type of nickname, places such as Newspaper Rock along Indian Creek on the way to Canyonland National Park, or the Newspaper Rock in Petrified Forest National Park, or Jailhouse Ruin in Bullet Canyon, Utah, or the Great Gallery pictograph panel in Utah, which has a shaman-like figure referred to as the Holy Ghost (Plate 43). Even the most descriptive names like the Green Mask site or the Quail panel tended to give the places and the rock art a tag, that is, the names tended to give a slant not only to my expectations but also to my experiences and eventual understanding of the places. What the names all had in common was their representation of an overlay or projection of how modern American culture comprehended these ancient places. Yet at the same time the names tended to confuse or interfere with other possible responses to the sites. Like electronic radar jamming, I somehow detected these names as a kind of jamming that occurred in the gap between myself and the place.

Unlike the graffiti contemporary American culture often leaves at rock art sites, this naming signifies an overlay onto the rock art that is difficult to ignore because it is invisible. Much like Columbus establishing dominion over newly discovered lands simply by naming them, identifications such as "the FBI panel" or "Newspaper Rock" served to establish a kind of psychological dominion over the rock art places. Seeing these places as newspaper rocks is analogous to seeing a huge hole in some large sandstone formation as "Paul Bunyon's Potty."

Contributing to this modern overlay is the fact that my brain is—at least to a considerable degree—"wired modern." Besides being transported to most sites in vehicles over modern paved or dirt roads with caches of freeze-dried food and guided by satellite-derived topographical maps, I know the modern site names (or numbers) and the current archeological thinking. I also know that the things making noise over my head are jet planes and I carry an 8″ × 10″ camera with which to make color photographic images. I know that I would not be able to survive on my own in any of the desert country in any of the states where I have traveled and backpacked. At the rock art sites this modern context is simply the latest layer of marks, and on the rock surfaces themselves it is represented by the graffiti or "defacement" such as "Butch Tangreen" (Fig. 3) or "D.V.H." or "M.J." (Plate 58). In a sense, this graffiti is simply the rock art of the modern context.

Beneath this modern layer, however, there are many earlier layers—drawings and hand prints and marks put onto the rocks through the centuries by people who evolved within an "indigenous context." At some sites the drawings are densely layered through time and as a consequence imply not only that the place was revisited over perhaps centuries but also that the petroglyph panel was created by many different individuals separated not by space but by time. At some sites the modern evidence is represented not only by the ubiquitous names, initials, and dates but also by other marks such as bullet holes that often occur where eyes should be (Plate 59). On the Comanche Gap hogback among numerous Anasazi petroglyphs there is even a—modern—flying saucer depiction!

As in any exploration, I worked from what I knew toward what I did not know. Like two arrows striking head on into each other, modern perceptions encountered not only prehistoric but also non-European images and symbols. Moreover, these pictographs and petroglyphs were entirely outside of my own cultural history and seemed as embedded in the landscape as my own perceptions were not. Since I was primarily interested in learning from, interacting with, and responding to the rock art sites this situation presented a conflict.

On the one hand I felt compelled to make photographs that were "accurate" descriptions in terms of a kind of topographical way of thinking, a mapping, really, of how the rock art is related to its surroundings. In the photograph of the star kachinas and Albuquerque, for example (Plate 60), the viewer can see, as of July 1983, the nearness of ancient marks to the modern city. I chose to work with an 8″ × 10″ camera primarily to be able to show detail within a large landscape. Most of the photographs that I have seen of rock art sites taken by archaeologists and other interested parties are cropped tight around the drawings with little or no view of the surrounding rock surfaces or landscape. I did not want the context to be completely sacrificed.

But what, exactly, is the context of rock art? Unlike many other cultural artifacts it still exists in the "real" world and not as a collected deposit in a modern museum or warehouse. In fact, a significant characteristic of rock art is that it seems integrally enclosed within a number of contexts, like something placed at the center of an expanding series of concentric circles. The inner circle or context would be the drawings and marks themselves and how they relate to each other, in a sense, the composition. This is usually determined, in part, by how the rock art is situated on the rock surface or surfaces upon which it is drawn, painted, pecked, or carved.

In the panel of petroglyphs at San Cristobal (Plate 50) a long, wavy "arrow-line" goes straight up through the middle of a smooth rock surface, a surface that is defined at the top by a subtle overhang. The arrow-line stops at this overhang. To remove this symbol from the context of the rock and place it in a "symbol inventory" along with other, similar symbols—as is done in much of the current rock art research—might have some comparative utility. But it also essentially defuses the symbol by removing it from not only the primary context of the other drawn elements (which in this case include two figures which seem to be chasing a turkey, two star-like symbols, a coyote head, and several faces and a large animal located around the corner from the main panel) but also from the secondary context of the rock itself.

Rock art also exists as human marks made on the land—as "landmarks"—which means that a broader context yet is that of the surrounding environment. The marks and drawings of any given site are configured in a relationship to each other, to the rocks upon which they are painted or pecked and to the surrounding space. Sometimes this space is a small niche such as that formed by the book-like pair of rock panels at McKee Springs in Utah (Plate 54); many times it is a canyon (Plate 45); often, as at Comanche Gap, the rock art is on a hogback or other vista location, and the surrounding space is not enclosed or delineated at all except in the broadest manner by distant mountains or other land features (Plates 46 and 47). Ultimately, all rock art sites are configured in relation to each other by how they are located in the landscape. Sites within canyons, such as the Barrier Canyon style of pictographs (Plates 43 and 59), are related to each other by a network of canyons and washes that all connect to the Green River like nerves to a spinal cord. Perhaps a majority of rock art sites are connected in terms of a watershed. Other sites, however, such as those on the hogbacks in the Galisteo Basin in New Mexico are in some sense related by the context of vision, by being in sight of each other. Another vista site such as Three Rivers in New Mexico, where the rock art is scattered on boulders along a two-mile-long hogback-like hump of land, seems to have been chosen because of its isolated position which is in sight of a large panorama of landmarks, including the 12,000-foot mountain peak Sierra Blanca (Plates 41 and 49).

The context of any given rock art drawing or mark ultimately is where it is located in terms of all that surrounds it, its *place* on the earth. As one can see in the photograph made in Hay Canyon, Utah (Fig. 3 with text), a place also exists under the conditions of change and of entropy, which means that the configuration of a rock art panel includes the context of time as well.

As I continued to visit rock art sites—many times on foot and often over great distances—I began to see them less as sites and more as places. My modern perceptions were oriented toward seeing the rock art in terms of sites that could be described. But I gradually grew less interested in the modern questions of "what do they mean" and "who made them" and, especially, "how old"; I began to perceive the rock art as having a more important function to me than to serve as the subject of my curious study. A site is something discrete and separate that can be objectively studied and photographed; it is the locus where some activity or event once occurred that is no longer occurring: it exists in the past

3. Historic, prehistoric, and entropy marks in Hay Canyon, Utah, October 16, 1982.

and we, as observers, are separate from it—it is the archaeological frame of reference. Topographical notions of photography can, perhaps, be applied to sites: they can, in some manner, be logically described because of their conceptual discreteness in time and space.

A place, however, is different; it exists within the flow of time—past, present, and future—and within the flow of space as well so that near and far are part of a continuum. A place is identifiable but, unlike a site, not separable from its surroundings. To try and describe a place is difficult, if not impossible, in the way that describing a dream or a nightmare is difficult: one is always confronted with the question of *how far back do you get, where do you place the frame?* Unlike a site, a place includes the observer as well, so that the configuration of a rock art place—its series of contexts that expand like concentric circles around a center—expands a notch further to include not only the surrounding land and time but also me, you, us. What this means, really, is that a photograph need not describe a rock art place at all but can work by analogy and can be a message of participation instead. A photograph can, perhaps, help one to identify with a place, to connect with it. The FBI panel becomes a place, metaphorically, for my (our) hand print as well.

Rock art, really, is a metaphor of connectedness. It was created by people who were, of necessity, an intimate part of their environment, their place on the earth, and it continues today as a kind of message that communicates that intimacy. Rock art places themselves function as landmarks that to me symbolize the connectedness or rootedness of the indigenous North American peoples.

For this "wired modern" white boy, rock art places represent a basic knowledge or "knowing" of the land that I grew up alienated from. The poet Gary Snyder speaks of the descendants of European cultures as invaders: "We haven't discovered North America yet. People live on it without knowing what it is or where they are. They live on it literally like invaders." He goes on to say that we will be inhabitants when we know well the plants that grow where we live. This metaphor suggests an intimacy with the land upon which we live that will lead, in time, to a feeling of sacredness about our place on earth. My visits to rock art places were simply opportunities—like many other opportunities, all of them important—to learn the lay of the land, to move in the direction of intimacy. The rock art places are like a series of teachings that are most fundamentally about being in places, not on or next to, not through them or separate from them, but about being in them, a part of the mystery.

As for the fires, they are a symbol of not only real time but also of my vision of belonging, and they represent the act of placing my hand, as in sympathetic magic, onto sacred places, not to hold or possess but to connect.

These photographs are one more layer, and I hope that they acknowledge and communicate my deep feelings for the special places that they depict.

41. Face commanding the space below Sierra Blanca, New Mexico, March 25, 1985.

42. A mask painted over a cave at Hueco Tanks, Texas, January 6, 1983.

43. Shaman-like figures in Horseshoe Canyon, Utah, June 1, 1983.

44. Anasazi petroglyphs and a small catch basin near the Galisteo River in New Mexico, January 6, 1985.

45. Fires and a four-sided boulder near Moab, Utah, June 8, 1983.

46. View north from atop the Comanche Gap hogback in New Mexico, July 14, 1983.

47. Looking east atop the Comanche Gap hogback in New Mexico, July 9, 1983.

Steve Fitch / 71

48. Night on top of Comanche Gap in New Mexico, December 22, 1982.

Steve Fitch / 72

49. Six-fingered hands at Three Rivers, New Mexico, July 1, 1983.

50. Dusk near San Cristobal ruin, New Mexico, August 9, 1984.

51. A ruin nicknamed "Moonhouse" in an unnamed canyon called "McLoyd's," Utah, June 17, 1983.

52. A small cave beside Katzima in New Mexico, August 18, 1984.

Steve Fitch / 76

53. Beside the campfire in southeastern Utah, October 12, 1982.

54. Sheltered fire and petroglyphs in eastern Utah, May 23, 1983.

Steve Fitch / 78

55. Shaman-like figures in the foothills of the Wind Rivers, Wyoming, November 19, 1982.

56. A fire and petroglyphs at dusk near San Cristobal ruin, New Mexico, July 28, 1983.

57. Fires beneath a possible breech birth depiction at Sheik Canyon, Utah, October 11, 1982.

58. Night fire at the Rochester Creek panel, Utah, October 14, 1984.

59. Campfire in Sego Canyon, Utah, October 4, 1984.

60. Star Kachinas above the city, New Mexico, July 23, 1983.

Elegy for the Drowned

John Pfahl

These photographs are of that which cannot be seen again. Pecked into smooth black boulders and embellishing large panels of rock, the petroglyphs that lie beneath the waters of New Mexico reservoirs provide a poignant footnote to the history of this most vulnerable form of mark making.

I have photographed rock drawings on many occasions, both before and since doing this work in the sunny, windy spring of 1984. I was attracted to their beauty, their eloquent mystery, and to the way in which they concretely defined sacred precincts in the vastness of the wilderness. By the very incompleteness of their statement and the unknowableness of their purpose, they seem to precipitate wandering speculations about nature, culture, and spirituality.

Chance would have it that the first book that came to hand when I arrived in Albuquerque for a year-long visit was *Rock Art in the Cochiti Reservoir District,* by Polly Schaafsma, with photographs by her husband, Curtis. What a joy to see those many pages filled with little faces, birds and deer, masked serpents, shield-men, and dancing figures! And then, what sadness to realize that I was holding all that remained of these spirited petroglyphs. The book was a report of archaeological salvage activities undertaken before the Rio Grande north of Albuquerque was dammed to form Cochiti Lake. The text, a fine example of neutral descriptive scientific writing, gave no indication of the emotions that the Schaafsmas may have had on their month-long field trip to the area in the fall of 1966.

I felt compelled to revisit the vicinity of these carefully documented sites as a kind of memorial pilgrimage. This was certainly not the usual way in which I approached my photographic projects. Hitherto, I had been drawn into a new concern by the spark of something visual. The appearance of a particular bend in the river at dawn, the possibilities of visual puns between mountains and vegetation, the symbolic reverberations of a man-made structure surrounded by the natural landscape—these were the things that inspired me to make photographs. In this case, however, my choices were already clearly spelled out in precise and technical detail, with site numbers, maps, and an

1. From *Rock Art in the Cochiti Reservoir District,* by Polly Schaafsma (Museum of New Mexico Press, Papers in Anthropology #16, 1967).

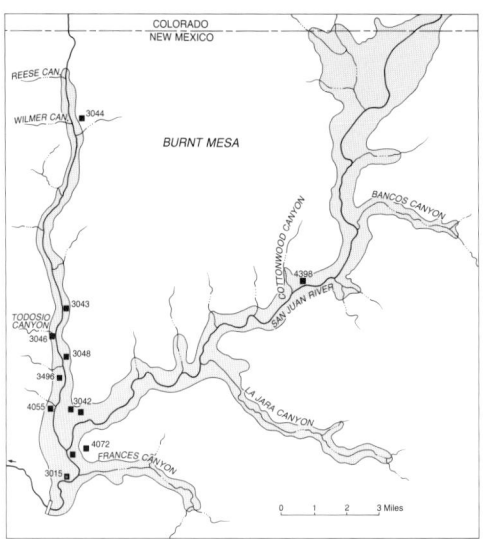

2. Map of the Navajo Reservoir District showing locations of Pueblo pictograph sites. From *Rock Art in the Navajo Reservoir District,* by Polly Schaafsma (Museum of New Mexico Press, Papers in Anthropology #7, 1963).

accumulation of other data. I had only to get to those vantage points overlooking the submerged archaeological sites and *receive* my picture. The unpredictability of the results of this procedure both intrigued and terrified me.

Cochiti Reservoir was built to control flooding and sedimentation and to provide recreational opportunities. Above the massive earthen dam, the eastern bank turned out to be fairly accessible by car and foot. My assistant Steve Federation and I were unable to follow the river-lake closely, however, due to many unnecessary detours around small side canyons. *LA 10116,* a site that appeared to be about four miles from the parking lot by map, was approached only after many hours of scrambling over cactus-covered sand and fields of hard boulders. The irony of trekking all that distance to photograph a spot on the lake that looked just minimally different from other (and more convenient) spots was not entirely lost on us. The site description, however, read:

> North of *LA 10115,* a long bench extends for almost a half mile before it is pinched out by steep talus slopes rising directly from the river banks. Petroglyphs were found only at the north end of the bench. At this point, the end of an old lava flow cuts above the talus slope above the bench, and from it, immense rhyolite boulders tumble down. Being slightly softer in character than the hard basalt we have dealt with so far, petroglyphs were more easily pecked into its rough surfaces. A horned serpent and large anthropomorphic figure, nearly three feet in height, are deeply carved in wide lines in a boulder high in the talus debris. The square body is decorated with lines of dots. The realistic depiction of the feet is unusual among Cochiti Reservoir figures.
>
> Other designs are pecked on boulders on the bench below. These include a masked serpent and a large shield figure, three feet high, lightly pecked and too faint to photograph. Of special interest is the profile head and large female figure with a rectangular body which resembles the anthropomorph higher up the talus slope.

As we stood above the silty lake trying to make out the approximate location of the small treasures of *LA 10116,* we were confronted only with placid swells of opaque water. We shuddered.

Other vantage points, on that and other crystalline days, proved to be easier to get to, but no less provocative. An aura seemed to insinuate itself between the perceived sites and our consciousness, so that we became convinced that we had indeed made contact, even if only elusively, with the figures themselves and with the ancient Pueblo tribesmen who had crafted them. I set out to photograph in other locales as well and followed the archaeological reports of rock art sites along the San Juan, Pine, and Chama rivers where now the Navajo and Abiquiu reservoirs gather their waters.

The Navajo Reservoir spreads itself out between the pine-covered mountains of northwestern New Mexico and crosses into Colorado, giving the appearance of a clear blue natural lake. I found easy access to the best vantage points in campsites and picnic grounds and along dirt roads leading to gas wells. This land had been inhabited for thousands of years, and most of the many rock drawings date from the Pueblo period (A.D. 700–1050) and the much later Navajo period (A.D. 1550–1775). As I aimed my view camera at the sparkling water, I felt surrounded by humpbacked fluteplayers, hunters, and animals, hand-holding anthropomorphs, planetariums of stars, flower forms, and numerous mythical beings. My invaluable guide here was Polly Schaafsma's earlier report, *Rock Art in the Navajo Reservoir District*.

From a photographer's point of view, which I had all but relinquished by this time, Abiquiu Reservoir was the loveliest of all. In an enormous valley northwest of Santa Fe surrounded by pink and red sandstone cliffs, the lake projected long fingers in all directions. The patterns of land and water were enticing. Here only a handful of sites had been found and surveyed, but they represented three separate cultures, superimposed like the surrounding rock strata. Drawings of large spearpoints and feathered shafts were left at *AR 26* by the ancient Pueblos, perhaps as early as 1300. The Spanish wrote inscriptions over them in 1758, and these, in turn, were covered by horses with bridles boldly pecked by the Utes or Pueblos who were in the area after the mid-eighteenth century.

It became increasingly clear to me that my melancholy quest was dedicated to all of the many petroglyphs and pictographs that had been lost to flood control, irrigation projects, looters and vandals, and the insensitive acts of unknowing tourists. Only the most inaccessible drawings have a chance to survive these ravages. Guarded by eagles and falcons, they still reveal themselves in untouched splendor to the intrepid backpacker.

Cannot these lost traces of ancient peoples also symbolize *all* the art and civilization, whether along the Nile, in the jungles of the Yucatan, or in the palaces of Venice, destroyed by the pillaging of time, war, progress, or natural disaster? Such were my ever-widening ruminations as I focused on the sad patches of water that betrayed not the slightest sign of the profusion of masks, animals, and tiny handprints submerged below.

61. Cochiti Reservoir, ". . . a masked serpent."

62. Cochiti Reservoir, ". . . small man carrying a large shield."

John Pfahl / 90

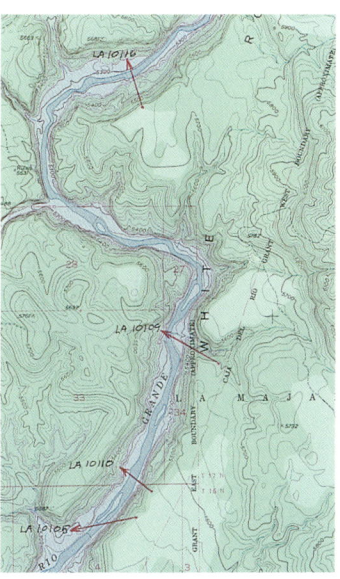

63. Cochiti Reservoir, ". . . a phallic male figure."

John Pfahl

64. Navajo Reservoir, ". . . horned-winged figure."

John Pfahl / 92

65. Navajo Reservoir, ". . . animals and small hand prints."

John Pfahl / 93

66. Abiquiu Reservoir, "Horses and men on horseback . . ."

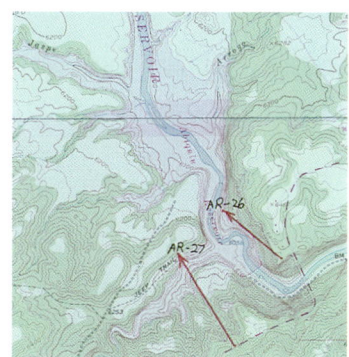

67. Abiquiu Reservoir, ". . . large spear points and some feathered shafts."

John Pfahl / 95

A Part of the Medium

Charles Roitz

As kingfishers catch fire, dragonflies draw flame;
As tumbled over rim in roundy wells
Stones ring; like each tucked string tells, each hung bell's
Bow swung finds tongue to fling out broad its name;
Each mortal thing does one thing and the same:
Deals out that being indoors each one dwells;
Selves—goes itself; myself it speaks and spells,
Crying "What I do is me: for that I came."

Gerard Manley Hopkins

Art making begins with intuitive knowledge and transforms it into an image. The sense of being, as Hopkins eloquently expresses it in the poem fragment above, is the object of my own art-making pursuit. I am fascinated by the possibility of extracting the essence of something and distilling it into a photograph that maintains the life force of the original. Photography, in my view, produces the best analogue of the subjects that attract me. For many years now, and more intensely in the last decade, I have photographed the landscape—the earth itself as well as plants, animals (including man), and the atmosphere. I have concentrated especially on the western part of the United States, but I have also worked recently in British Columbia, Italy, and Peru, seeking those marks man has made on the land that give a sense of place and reveal something about the individuals and groups who made them. From 1976 to 1982 I produced a body of photographs entitled "Towards a Contemporary Consciousness," specifically attempting to contextualize in the landscape those marks made by man since the advent of the Industrial Revolution. My photographic activity shifted in 1982 with the funding of the National Endowment for the Arts Photographic Survey Project "Marks and Measures, Pictographs and Petroglyphs in a Modern Art Context." This was an opportunity to photograph the traces of ancient inhabitants, of indigenous peoples whose writing was in the form of pictures rather than words.

The context of an image has become a central issue in my recent work. No marks exist in isolation; to the contrary they exist and gain their full meaning only when seen in relation to all that surrounds them. Physical location is one aspect of the context, and certainly it determines where one places the camera, what is included as relevant, and the balance or lack of it that one perceives. But this is only part of a complex issue; other elements are perhaps even more important, at least to me. The more important elements have to do with seeing through to the

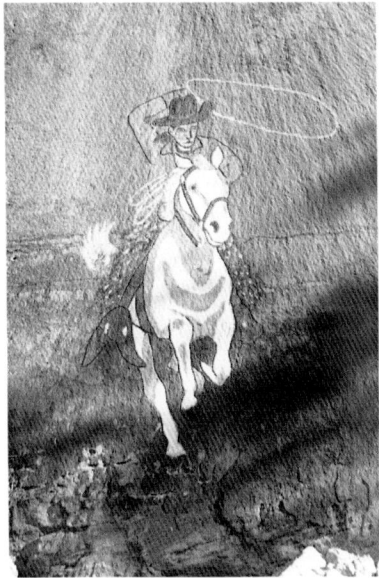  

1. Cowboy, Colorado, 1960.   2. Indian, Colorado, 1960.   3. Eagle, Colorado, 1960.

essence of the marks. In making an image, my primary goal is to record something beyond the physical characteristics of object and place, organized intuitively in an appropriate form.

My first experiences with a rock art site in 1958 and 1960 were formative ones and help to illuminate my position. After a brief visit to the small, partially ruined stone house where Martin Bowden had lived as a hermit for many years, friends and I descended into Picketwire Canyon, which had been carved out of sandstone by the Purgatory River. To my astonishment, on the canyon wall were all the technicolor characters I had become accustomed to seeing on the movie screen on Saturday afternoons while growing up in Trinidad, Colorado, thirty miles to the west. On one wall was a larger-than-life cowboy, fully costumed, lariat whirling, coming directly at me on a galloping white horse. Behind a tree, partially hidden in shadow, was a classic American Indian portrait, head and shoulders, three-quarter view. Descending from a high cliff face, an American bald eagle was prepared to snatch a small rodent from the canyon floor. The buffalo was there, as was Wild Bill Hickcock and many exotic creatures, such as a smiling Bengal tiger. I was fascinated that someone had lived alone in the desert and had made these images—but I also remember being disappointed that they were well-worn, shallow Hollywood characterizations.

My second trip to the site was more productive. By that time I suspected that a precedent for Martin's image-making in this canyon was the rock art of ancient peoples. At the time, however, I was totally unprepared for what I would find. Local history, even that provided by folklore, began only with the Spanish inhabitants. There were no Indians left, and very little evidence of them that I knew of, only a few arrowheads. To my delight I found ancient images pecked on the rocks at the base of the cliffs that Martin had used for his paintings. They were heavily weathered and abstract, distinctly unrelated to Bowden's "realistic" images. But, to me, the ancient images conveyed more *realism* than Martin's "cartoons"—the *crawl* of a snake, the *radiation* of a heavenly body. The ancient artist knew how to abstract the essence of form and depict it in these marks.

4. Tiger, Colorado, 1960.

I am convinced, as was Hopkins, that there is something beyond physicality. In the second and last stanza of his poem, Hopkins talks about spiritual connectedness—that is, incorporeal relationships. For him the relationship with a Christian God was important. In examining the art of prehistoric non-Christians, I found evidence of both physical life and spiritual life. All of the practical physical events one might expect were there—hunting, tilling the soil, transportation of materials, and so on—but the images of nonphysical events held special interest for me.

At sites in all of the countries I visited, depictions of the effort to escape the physical body were numerous and powerful. The most interesting for me were those that dealt with anthropomorphism, metamorphosis, and shamanism. Costuming, masking, and music/dance rituals were, to me, the signs of attempts at transcendence and were the most evocative for my art-making purposes.

Most of the rock art showed extensively the effects of weather and plant and animal activity. I included these elements in the photographs because it was almost impossible not to, but also because they indicate the present condition of the marks and the passage of time in a wonderfully complex and active landscape.

In an attempt to call as little attention to myself and to the photographic medium in these images, I used the 8 × 10 format to capture every detail of this elusive subject matter and long-familiar black and white materials in a straightforward way. I wanted to allow the ancient marks and the landscape to imprint themselves on film, passing on as clearly as possible to the viewer. The necessary choices I made were primarily intuitive and were purposefully effected with a gentle, quiet hand. In this work I feel more a part of the medium than in a position of artistic ownership.

In our busy city lives we have few opportunities for direct experience with much of the natural world. There are opportunities, however where we can participate through a ritual in the long history of human experience. One such opportunity came for me a few years ago at Midnight Mass at San Felipe Pueblo, New Mexico. The experience paralleled that of photographing for this project. After the priest had celebrated mass, with all its prescriptions properly and elegantly executed, he announced that "now it is time for nature." Drums began to beat rhythmically and to everyone's surprise and delight, native dancers in full animal costume made their pulsating way down the central aisle. Each dancer combined the rhythm of the animal whose skin or feathers he wore with his own natural rhythm. The sense of continuity that had been important to me while photographing in canyons, deserts, rain forest, glacial moraine, and cloud forest was present in this midnight mass dance; anthropomorphism, metamorphosis, shamanism, costuming, masking, music and dance were all part of this two-culture ritual, and they seemed to connect me to ancient peoples and their petroglyphs in an important way.

Photography, like religious performance rituals can be an efficient medium for transcendant experience. Perhaps this book makes that clear.

68. Untitled, Rio Abiseo National Park, Peru, 1985.

69. Untitled, Rio Abiseo National Park, Peru, 1985.

70. Untitled, Rio Abiseo National Park, Peru, 1985.

71. Untitled, Rio Abiseo National Park, Peru, 1985.

72. Untitled, British Columbia, Canada, 1983.

Charles Roitz / 104

73. Untitled, British Columbia, Canada, 1983.

74. Untitled, British Columbia, Canada, 1983.

Charles Roitz / 106

75. Untitled, Washington, 1982.

76. Untitled, Utah, 1982.

77. Untitled, Utah, 1982.

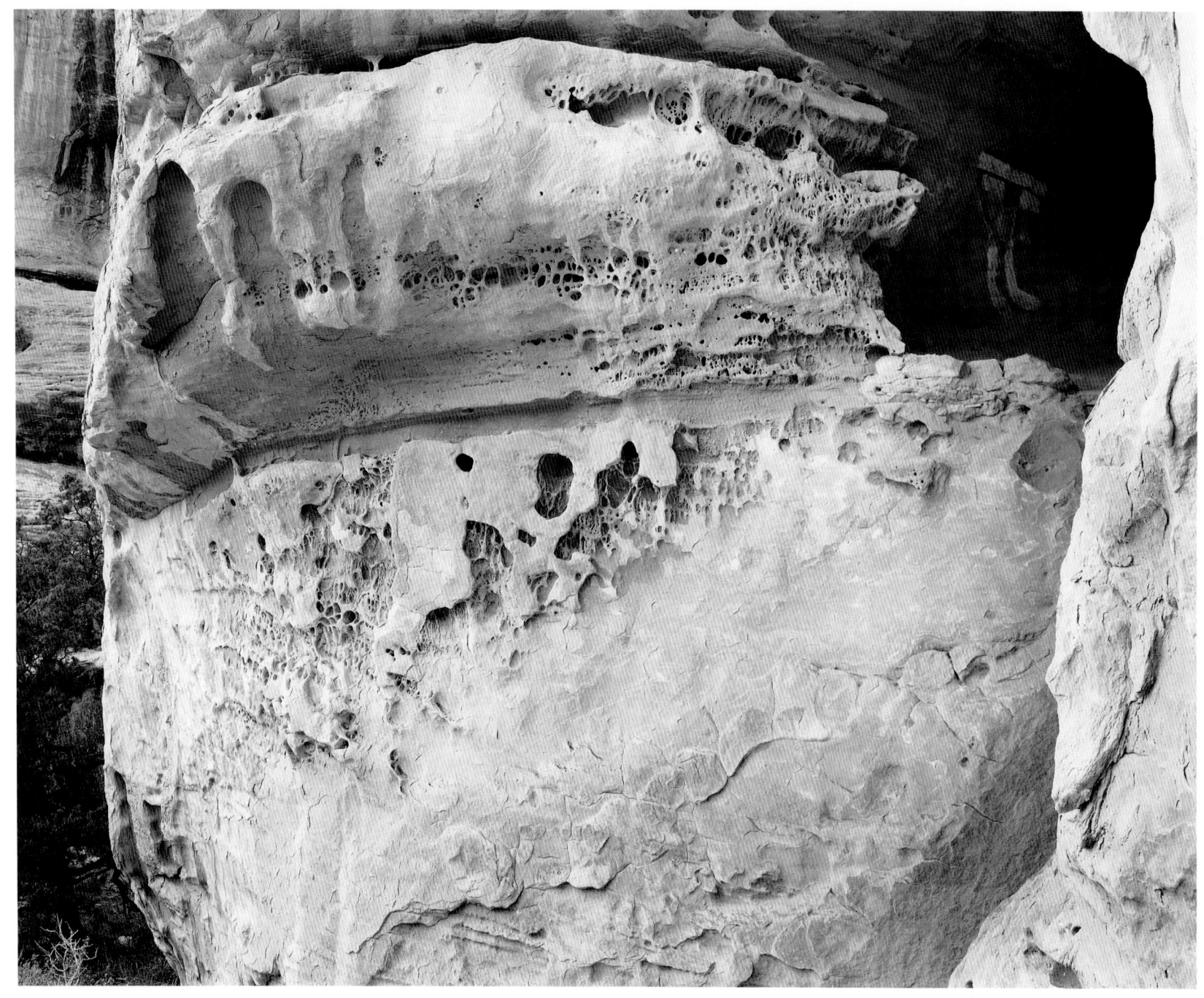

78. Untitled, Utah, 1982.

79. Untitled, Wyoming, 1983.

80. Untitled, Utah, 1983.

81. Untitled, Texas, 1983.

82. Untitled, Utah, 1984.

83. Untitled, Utah, 1984.

84. Untitled, Texas, 1983.

85. Untitled, Valcamonica, Italy, 1985.

86. Untitled, Utah, 1983.

87. Untitled, Utah, 1983.

Modernism and the Quest for Primacy

Keith Davis

The question needs to be asked. In our predominantly secular, scientific, and skeptical age, what relevance could these "primitive" marks have for some of our leading contemporary artists? This pointed and sensible question is not easily answered, as analysis leads all too quickly to a seemingly endless range of issues, influences, traditions, and values. However, it is this writer's opinion that the works illustrated in this book are important to an understanding of the broadest currents of contemporary thought. Such works may be considered particular to the last decade or two of contemporary photography, as well as a logical part of the entire Western, modernist tradition.[1] The following essay suggests a few of these connections, and the attitudes implicit in them. However cursory, this effort touches on our philosophic and artistic heritage, the meaning of—and reactions to—our prevailing Western world view, and the relationship of contemporary artistic thought to notions of religion and time.

In recent years the ideas of Robert Smithson, books such as Lucy Lippard's *Overlay,* and exhibitions such as the Museum of Modern Art's *"Primitivism" in Twentieth-Century Art* have represented important aspects of the deep appeal primal images hold for contemporary artists. On examination, this appeal reveals much about the dilemmas and utopian longings of the modern psyche, and of our collective need for a sense of rootedness. The attraction of these primal marks stems from a richly complex set of themes and ideas, including a nostalgia for collective systems and shared beliefs; a new interest in myth, ritual and magic; a critique of the dominant Judeo-Christian, Cartesian, and scientific world views; an aesthetic interest in "art" by those outside the modernist, academic tradition; a fascination, stemming from linguistic theory, with signs and symbols; and our attitudes toward time and history.

These ancient marks are seen by many to represent the innocent infancy of human consciousness and the enduring relics of a proud, lost race. While existing in physical and archeological fact, these marks are most significant to us as self-created symbols functioning as mute vessels to be filled with our longings, dreams, and notions of artistic and personal value. Their perceived magic and sacred aura stem from their ability to focus our own projected needs. Through their mystery and elemental presence these marks serve to suggest the latent powers of magic, sacredness, and transcendence that (we hope) lie within us.

The experience of visiting and photographing rock art sites can be intensely private and deeply moving. Since they are often found in distant or infrequently visited areas, the search for rock art can often resemble an act of pilgrimage or ascetic retreat. Viewers often comment that the sites have an inherent human appeal owing to the physical qualities of the place itself or its relationship to the surrounding topography. The sites also represent an extraordinary integration of art with the world. Far removed from the neutral environment of the museum, rock art sites provide a powerful aesthetic experience within the ever changing environmental conditions of heat, cold, wind, rain, sunlight, or darkness. To the sensitive viewer, therefore, the aesthetic aura that we reserve to art may be perceived as having radiated out from the object itself, permeating the entire world and charging it with new mystery and meaning. The stillness and apparent timelessness of the petroglyphs merge with our awareness both of nature's presence and energy, and of our own fragile being. These hand-hewn marks—often so few and small within a seemingly boundless landscape—present a powerful image of a balanced relationship between culture and nature, and between human and geologic time. The anonymous nature of these marks suggests their function as pure *cultural* expressions, as evidence of the conceptual bonds among people, and between human communities and the earth. And, from a self-reflexive, modernist viewpoint, photographs of these marks represent artistic meditations on the most primal qualities—marking and symbol-making—of art itself.

The current fascination with primal marks stems in part from a belief in the unity of all experience, subjective as well as objective, and a revolt against the perceived artificiality and alienation of modern society. For the purposes of discussion, the modern expression of these ideas may be said to have arisen in the Romantic movement of the late eighteenth and early nineteenth centuries. The Romantics rejected rationalism, stability, and industrialism and felt inspired by what was grand, remote, terrifying, or ancient. In both painting and literature this interest was frequently expressed in images of ruins which celebrated the melancholy grandeur of time and decay, and the poignant smallness of man's works.

Rousseau, the progenitor of the Romantic movement, celebrated a "Natural Religion" in which Truth was sensed emotionally rather than intellectually. Likewise, Wordsworth felt that the important facts of nature eluded the scientific method and were available only by way of feeling, while William Blake perceived the entire world, including the observer, as a "primal and eternal unity."[2] While Romanticism had a deep interest in ancestry and "blood consciousness,"[3] it was, at root, deeply antisocial. Its goal was the liberation of an heroicized Self from the fetters of social convention and mundane practicality. To an important degree, Romanticism's mixture of transcendence, narcissism, and alienation established the primary themes of the modern era.

Some of the leading nineteenth-century philosophers extended certain aspects of Romanticism's inherent subjectivity. Kant, for example, considered the things of the world unknowable in isolation and stressed the interaction of the observer's perceptual/cognitive faculties and the objects of the physical world. Similarly, Hegel's early interest in mysticism led him to a faith in the unity of all things. For him, the whole in all its complexity was the Absolute, a spiritual force which permeated the cosmos. Schopenhauer was very sympathetic to notions of ascetic mysticism, spiritualism, and magic, and preferred Eastern religions to Christianity. Schopenhauer's unifying concept was that of the Will, a timeless, universal force inherent in all things. Ideas of separateness and individuality were, for him, illusions created by the subjectivity of spatiotemporal perception.

Nietzsche, like Schopenhauer, felt "the tremendous awe which seizes man when he suddenly begins to doubt the cognitive modes of experience."[4] While Nietzsche's ideas were largely based on notions of power and human inequality, he too described his particular vision of a "complete oneness with the essence of the universe."[5] Nietzsche celebrated the "Dionysiac rapture" in which the individual forgets himself under the influence of "narcotic potions" or the potency of spring. Nietzsche wrote, "Not only does the bond between man and man come to be forged once more by the magic of the Dionysiac rite, but nature itself, long alienated or subjected, rises again to celebrate the reconciliation with her prodigal son, man."[6]

A similar wariness of Positivistic certainty typifies the philosophy of Henri Bergson and William James. Bergson valued intuition over reason because it preserved the underlying wholeness of life rather than artificially dividing the world into separate things. Reality, for Bergson, was a singular process of becoming—a process that united perception and memory, since it is in memory that the past survives in, and interpenetrates, the present. William James strove to abolish the Cartesian dualism between mind and matter, intellect and feeling. James felt that logical analysis and reduction were, in themselves, fundamentally distorting and that all facets of experience—including dreams, visions, hallucinations, feelings, faith, and perceptions—were equally "real." For James, magic, religion, and science were all theories or systems of knowledge, frames of reference for understanding the world.

The perceived complexities of nature and the mind were extended in the first decades of the twentieth century. In physics Einstein and Heisenberg posited the interrelationships of matter and energy, motion and time, the observer and the observed. The concepts of relativity and the uncertainty principle denied the assumptions of Positivistic science and the notion of "objective" perception. This unsettling interpretation of the relation between man and the world was paralleled by Freud's path-breaking studies of the unconscious, which rendered the mechanical view of the mind increasingly untenable. While he retained his own faith in the importance of rational thought, Freud's work suggested the vast depths of an alien and "primitive" mental world. His work gave new meaning to the concepts of dreams, instincts, and symbols while calling into question the presumed superiority of ideas over feelings, intent over instinct, and reason over energy.

The study of myths arose in tandem with this new picture of the mind. Sir James Frazier's highly influential *The Golden Bough* linked "primitive" magic and religious thought to contemporary institutions and folk customs. Frazier recognized the function of myths as unifiers of experience, and contributed to the belief that myths "lie within us . . . life is a steady mythical identification, a procession in the footsteps of others, a sacred repetition."[7]

Ernst Cassirer's thoughts on myth combined the influence of Frazier's studies with those of Einstein and Heisenberg. Cassirer felt that modern rationality and skepticism ultimately collapsed on themselves as theoretical and scientific knowledge was recognized only as evidence of the structure of our perceptual and cognitive structures. In this self-reflexive hall of mirrors, myth and spiritual feelings become newly valuable—in addition to language, science, and art—as direct "*organs* of reality, since it is solely by their agency that anything real becomes an object for intellectual apprehension, and as such is made visible to us. The question of what reality is apart from these forms, and what are its independent attributes becomes irrelevant. . . ."[8]

Such myths form the basis for Jung's studies of universal archetypes and the collective unconscious. Archetypes, in Jung's view, are "universal images" embodying primal motifs such as birth, fertility, and the daily or seasonal cycles. The content of an archetype, while unconscious in itself, is flavored by being brought to consciousness and expressed in the legends, rituals, or customs of a particular group. Through these expressions myths constitute the living religion—the very psychic life—of a tribe or group.

Like philosophers and writers, visual artists of the modern era have also sought to express their feelings for myths, suprahuman absolutes, and the unity of all things. Artists from at least Gauguin to the present have explored the relationship of the individual to him- or herself, the group, and the cosmos by way of mythic, ritualistic, and "primitive" motifs. This interest in alien cultures or the distant past signals a search for roots and rebirth in which Truth is sought in its original simplicity. For all these artists a sense of identity with something larger than the individual is essential, whether it be nature, geometry, or the fecund depths of the irrational mind.

The artists of the Symbolist movement explored the nonrational realms of imagination and fantasy. Their art projected the sensations of feeling onto nature in order to express a dreamlike unity of self and world. Gauguin exemplified the basic tenants of the Symbolist ideal by valuing the need to work freely and intuitively, sensation over analytical thought, inner essences over outward appearances, and memory over direct observation. Gauguin's move from France to Tahiti represented his search for a utopian, primal world and a "harmony between human life and that of animals and plants" in which "the deep voice of the earth [could] play an important part" in his work.[9]

The Symbolist critic Aurier echoed this need for intuition over analysis. He decried the effects of the natural sciences by stating that "it is mysticism that we need today, and it is mysticism alone that can save our society from brutalization, sensualism, and utilitarianism. . . ."[10] For Aurier, art was "simple, spontaneous and primordial," an expression of "emotivity" so basic that it "makes the soul tremble."[11] The idea that true understanding—and artistic creation—is derived from intuitive rather than rational inquiry is a fundamental aspect of modernist ideology. Alfred Stieglitz stated the position succinctly when he said, "When I am no longer thinking, but simply *am,* then I may be said to be truly affirming life. Not to *know,* but to let exist what is, that alone, perhaps, is truly to know."[12] James Ensor, in a speech in 1923, stated flatly that "reason is the enemy of art. Artists dominated by reason lose all feeling, powerful instinct is enfeebled, inspiration becomes impoverished and the heart lacks its rapture. . . ."[13] Jean Arp wrote that his aim was "to destroy the rationalist swindle for man and incorporate him again humbly in nature."[14] Similarly, Kandinsky felt that knowledge of things produced a gradual "disenchantment" in which the world lost its aura and mystery.[15]

The denial of the individual ego was also seen by many artists as essential to artistic insight. For Mondrian, it was important that the artist free "himself from individual sentiments" and break "loose from the domination of the individual inclination within him."[16] Marsden Hartley went so far as to say, "I prefer to have no personal life. Personal art is for me a matter of spiritual indelicacy."[17] In 1934 Edward Weston celebrated

> the mechanical camera and indiscriminate lens-eye, [which] by restricting too personal interpretation, directs the worker's course toward an impersonal revealment of the objective world. "Self-expression" is an objectification of one's deficiencies and inhibitions. In the discipline of camera technique, the artist can become identified with the whole of life.[18]

Similarly, Brancusi felt that "there is a purpose in everything. In order to achieve it, one must detach oneself from an awareness of self. I am no longer of this world, I am far from myself, I am no longer a part of my own person. I am within the essence of things themselves."[19]

This image of residing "within the essence of things themselves" can best be understood as a metaphor for religious feeling. In fact, the links between modern art and mystic or spiritualistic beliefs are numerous: in the secular and skeptical age of the twentieth century, art becomes an important window on the inexplicable, and a metaphysical system in itself. The act of creation becomes a central metaphor for this art: Klee described art as a "simile for Creation,"[20] while Picasso wrote that "the important thing is to create. Nothing else matters; creation is all."[21] Franz Marc, in 1914–15, wrote that "this art is our religion, our center of gravity, our truth," adding that "the art of our epoch will undoubtedly show profound analogies with the arts of long past, primitive times."[22] And, in 1947, Mark Rothko stated that a picture "must be miraculous . . . a revelation, an unexpected and unprecedented resolution of an eternally familiar need."[23] Here we sense the paradox of artistic Self and selflessness, as artists portray themselves as both Everyman and Creator, as an egoless eye and the maker of miracles.

The direct influence of "primitive" art and artifacts on Western avant-garde artists was made possible by the establishment of important ethnographic museums in the last third of the nineteenth century. This influence found tentative expression in the work of Gauguin and had a major impact in 1906–7 with the interest in African and Oceanic objects by Picasso, Matisse, Derain, and Vlaminck. In subsequent years a rapid change in artistic taste brought increased recognition of "primitive" objects as both "art" and meaningful symbols of the integration of individual, society, and cosmos felt to be lacking in the "civilized" cultures. The incorporation of these objects into the framework of Western aesthetic thought was made possible by the philosophic and artistic traditions cited above, and changing attitudes toward the fate of colonial peoples.

At this time many artists began looking to the past or to distant cultures for visions of primacy, innocence, and the aura of faith. It is necessary to emphasize the profound appeal of both "primitive" art itself, and the *idea* of primal man. The Western world after the Great War was, in the minds of many artists and intellectuals, anemic, decadent, and exhausted. Oswald Spengler's pessimistic book *The Decline of the West* (1918) symbolized the era's feelings of disillusionment. Not surprisingly, then, the remote past became for many artists a utopia of purity, vitality, and hope. Kandinsky, for example, wrote that "the further into the past we look, the fewer deceptions and sham works we find. They have mysteriously disappeared. Only the genuine artistic beings remain. . . ."[24] The Futurists, who were such aggressive proponents of the machine age, could still see themselves as "the primitives of a completely renovated sensitiveness."[25] And Malevich wrote that "the Suprematist square and the forms proceeding out of it can be likened to the primitive marks (symbols) of aboriginal man which represented, in their combinations, *not ornament but a feeling of rhythm.*"[26] DeChirico reveals some envy as he writes that "original man must have wandered through a world of uncanny signs. He must have trembled at every step."[27]

Later, during the tumultuous years of World War II and the Cold War, the Abstract Expressionist painters were also attracted to the example of primitive art and a heroic interpretation of primal man. Their sense of identity as inheritors of a particularly American notion of (Manifest) destiny provided a natural sympathy for the arts of the "primitive" Native Americans. For example, Adolf Gottlieb had seen the art of American Indians in 1937 and admired its vocabulary of simple, primal forms, while Jackson Pollock compared his own working method with that of the Indian sand painters. For the Abstract Expressionists the primal represented vast space, deep time, and the merger of the Self with the cosmos. In a manifesto published in 1943 Gottlieb and Rothko stated that "there is no such thing as a good painting about nothing. We assert that the subject is crucial and only that subject-matter is valid which is tragic and timeless. That is why we profess spiritual kinship with primitive and archaic art."[28] As Robert Motherwell stated in 1951, it was understood that "the art of far more ancient and 'simple' artists expressed . . . a feeling of *already* being at one with the world."[29] For alienated artists in a competitive society, this vision of wholeness was nothing short of Edenic.

Barnett Newman's 1947 article "The First Man Was An Artist" posits a heroic source, expressed in the Existential vocabulary of the day, for his own artistic generation. Newman states that "undoubtedly the first man was an artist," and goes on to say that "the necessity for dream is stronger than any utilitarian need. . . . Man's first expression, like his first dream, was an aesthetic one. . . . Original man, shouting his consonants, did so in yells of awe and anger at his tragic state, at his own self-awareness, and at his own helplessness before the void."[30] Art, in Newman's view, was the first human creation, and expressed the timeless but fundamentally absurd and tragic relationship between man and the cosmos. As such, art expressed truths that were unavailable to purely rational modes of inquiry.

> . . . The artist today is striving for a closer approach to the truth concerning original man than can be claimed by the paleontologist, for it is the poet and the artist who are concerned with the function of original man and who are trying to arrive at his creative state. What is the *raison d'etre*, what is the explanation of the seemingly insane drive of man to be painter and poet if it is not an act of defiance against man's fall and an assertion that he will return to the Adam of the Garden of Eden? For the artists are the first men.[31]

The art of the 1960s and 1970s focused increasingly on the notion of unity as the locus of artistic activity shifted from the studio to the world. The rigorous puritanism of Minimal art, for example, is centered in the simplicity of primary forms and perceptual wholeness. Carl Andre was reputedly canoeing on a lake in New Hampshire when he decided that his sculpture should be as level—and presumably as natural, whole, and mysterious—as water. Such works denied the rationalizing powers of words and theories (at least in theory!) in favor of pure presence, and a timeless sensibility that blurred the present into the infinite. Suzi Gablik has written on Minimalism that

> the self-sufficient language of the grid . . . remains as nothing less than a kind of Rosetta stone for our age, the significance of whose code has not really been broken.[32]

The environmental works of the late 1960s and 1970s drew from the oversized studio gestures of Abstract Expressionism, the cerebral precision of Minimalism, and the physicality of Performance art. The art of Robert Smithson, Walter de Maria, Michael Heizer, and others reflects an important set of shared concerns. By greatly enlarging the scale of previous work these artists emphasized the small size (but presumably large ambitions) of man, while their involvement with the earth and natural processes stressed a new attitude toward time and change. Many of these works required viewers to travel long distances to experience them, thus engaging their audience in an entirely different way than readily accessible gallery art. The Minimalist interest in primary forms is seen in most of these works, which carry little narrative save for the scale, weight, and presence of the aesthetic "thing itself." In their mystery and silence these works seek to reinvent the world of both aesthetic experience and cultural meaning.

The influence of premodern Peruvian and Native American earth works on many of these artists illustrates our contemporary search for artistic vitality or intuitive wholeness in "outsider" art forms. These include "primitive" or tribal arts as already noted, as well as nonacademic Western forms such as folk art and graffitti. Folk art draws its special appeal primarily from its presumed naive and timeless themes, its rootedness in faith and fantasy, and its compulsive, seemingly unselfconscious creation. Folk art satisfies our longing for contemporary ritual objects that, at the same time, suggest an ageless creative impulse. The celebration of graffitti as both object and art is similarly motivated; the characteristic anonymity of such works suggests an "archetypal" creative impulse that we find attractive.

Related to these ideas is the impact of twentieth-century linguistic theory on our notions of signs and signifiers. The work of Saussure, Lacan, Barthes, and others describes the sign, expression, or narrative as a complex abstraction with its own internal logic and endless permutations of meaning. Oddly enough, this approach seems in philosophic agreement with the biblical Genesis: both are posited on the belief that "in the beginning was the Word." That is, human culture is understood to stem from man's ability to communicate through written or verbal signs and symbols. The simple "sign," then, becomes an emblem of cultural primacy and a representation of basic human creativity. The *mark* in and of itself becomes a potent symbol of the human presence. The interest of photographers in such emblems is extensive and includes (to name only two) Brassai's photographs of graffitti in the 1930s and 1940s, and Walker Evans's deep interest in American vernacular signs and folk imagery.

The dominant Western rational view of reality has come under increasing attack in the twentieth century by a wide variety of writers, philosophers, and artists. The various forms of this critique focus on the limits of the scientific method in providing sustaining values, and the split between knowledge and belief, analysis and belonging. In the first half of this century, for example, Yeats sought to reanimate a world that he felt to be deadened by the rationalistic, scientific legacy of the Enlightenment. Yeats sought a healthier integration of man and the cosmos through the occult, Romanticism, and the supernatural. He sought to reawaken the living quality of the world which the fragmenting, analytic attitude of science had denied. Yeats looks nostalgically back to a "golden, organic, pre-scientific age of faith or myth" before thought had become rationalized and life industrialized.[33]

Yeats's vision is echoed in books such as Morris Berman's *The Reenchantment of the World,* which argues that the falseness of our current world view resides in its split between fact and value. Prior to the scientific revolution, Berman states, the entire world was seen as an enchanted place of belonging and identity with nature—a place of psychic wholeness. The modern epoch, by contrast, is represented by an extreme separation from nature, and a rationalistic, alienated, valueless, disenchanted world view in which meaninglessness and violence dominate our lives.

The roots of this disenchantment lie in the Enlightenment and scientific revolution, when "how?" replaced "why?" as the question culture chose to ask of the world. This replacement of *value* by *fact* was expressed in Descarte's emphasis on the body-mind split, and a scientific methodology that treated nature mechanistically, as a thing to be disassembled and known in abstraction. Man's relationship to the world shifted, therefore, from one of integral belonging to one of knowledge through fragmentation and impersonal "laws." As Keith Thomas observes in *Man and the Natural World,* the rejection by seventeenth-century scientists of a man-centered symbolism represented a new detachment and objectivity, a realization of the natural world's "disinterest" in the human world. The significance of this disinterest is suggested by Robbe-Grillet, who wrote that, while the faith in knowing nature's secrets gave man the "power of dominion over the world," now we can "no longer consider the world as our very own, our private property, designed according to our needs and readily domesticated. . . . Man looks out at the world, and the world does not return his glance."[34]

This secular, disenchanted world view reflects altered notions of time (from cyclical to linear), nature (organic to mechanistic), and religion (from faith to skepticism). The modern rise of capitalistic economies, with their emphasis on the abstractions of money, accumulation, and power, further disrupted the fabric of thought in existence through the medieval period. In sum, this revolution in thinking represented the progressive removal of mind or spirit from the objects of the world.

According to Berman, the Western world's last attempt at a mystical and participatory understanding of nature lay in the practice of alchemy. The medieval alchemist, in this view, "did not *confront* matter; he *permeated* it."[35] While modern science may be seen as the secular remnant of the alchemist's dream to understand and transform nature, it holds the mistaken notion that inquiry can be disinterested and "value-free." Thus, it can only perceive the world as fragmentary, inert, and distant. But, Berman argues, impersonal and objective knowledge is meaningless, since all knowledge involves *meaning* and the reciprocal relationship of the knower and the known.

For its critics, this rationalistic, mechanistic, Cartesian model of the alienated consciousness has been increasingly invalidated by modern physics. Contemporary notions of relativity and the subjectivity of all experience seem to point away from Newtonian cause and effect toward Eastern religious thought and premodern mysticism. Such beliefs emphasize the inclusion of the observer in the things observed, the mystical connectedness of all things, and the inability of the intellect to comprehend things of real significance. This holistic outlook denies the exclusive authority of modern science while stressing the inseparability of fact and value (rather than "value-free" inquiry); the contextual nature of knowledge (rather than knowledge by way of dissection and isolation); the ultimate goals of wisdom, beauty, and grace (rather than those of control and repression); and a circular, ritualistic sense of time (rather than linear time and the notion of infinite progress).

These basic concepts are echoed in books such as Jamake Highwater's *The Primal Mind,* which examines the schism between the conceptual paradigms of the "civilized" and "primal" world views. Highwater stresses that it is not facts and objectivity but rather the visionary and aesthetic which provide genuine knowledge. He traces Western notions of primal people from the time of Rousseau, when the "savage" was deemed "noble" by virtue of being unspoiled by civilization. The pristine "otherness" of such peoples came to represent an escape from the rigid hierarchy of Western values and mores. "The West has grown positively sick of looking at itself, and it is trying to catch a dim glimpse of some vague 'otherness,' some potential alternative, some different reality previously hidden beyond the self-congratulatory mirrors of a stifled and windowless civilization."[36] In Highwater's view, the West is undergoing a spiritual crisis because "Western society no longer has a viable, functioning myth. It therefore has no basis to affirm life."[37] From this perspective, primal art represents a sacred trust for mankind.

> The Stone Age murals found on the walls of caves in Spain and France constitute the fragile but significant continuum of human consciousness. Altimira is a reservoir of a spiritual mentality which . . . has survived to revivify our humanity when it seems in its moment of greatest peril. . . . Altimira represents that sacredness of place and that perennial reality of the now which primal peoples have always understood as the first principle of their existence.[38]

Stones, according to Jung, possess a particular power for man in and of themselves, even before they become the bearers of primal marks. Jung wrote of stones as symbols for the Self, each one distinct and mute, "as if the stones held a living mystery," and were "containers of the life-force." Stones symbolize the "experience of something eternal that man can have in those moments when he feels immortal and unalterable."[39] In Jung's view it was this feeling that motivated primitive cultures to create stone monuments as signs and totems. He notes that religious cults frequently use stones to signify God or to mark a sacred place, and that in the Bible, Christ is referred to as a "rock." Even in their unhewn form stones were often seen by "primitive" societies as the dwelling places of spirits or Gods, or as mediators between man and the eternal.

The religious aspects of rock art and the power it holds for contemporary artists are suggested in the writings of Mircea Eliade. According to Eliade modern man perceives the "primitive" as engaged in a mystical participation in his world that suggests a universal animism. This, in turn, implies the very foundations of the religious or spiritual experience. In the nineteenth century—a period obsessed with the search for origins and primary causes—it was believed that religious faith passed through discrete stages of historical development, from animism to polytheism to monotheism. With the "death" of the monotheistic God, it is not surprising that the search for spiritual solace has led back in time and out in space toward "the primordial, original, universal *matrix.*"[40]

There are numerous aspects of the artistic experience of primal marks that evoke a fundamentally religious orientation. The majority of rock art sites are reached only by some physical effort, particularly for those carrying large view cameras and equipment. The process of finding these sites, as noted before, becomes a form of pilgrimage that is repeated—always the same, ever different—across hundreds of miles and, in some cases, over entire continents.

Further, many rock art sites are located in the ascetic environment of the desert. As Paul Shepard has noted, "the desert is the environment of revelation, genetically and physiologically alien, sensorily austere, esthetically abstract, historically inimical."[41] The desert is an environment that historically and psychologically evokes images of pilgrimage, hallucination, boundlessness, and spiritual enlightenment. The great Western religions began in the dessicated lands of the Middle East where, it might be suggested, intense light, immense space, and physical and psychic deprivation all contributed to new kinds of vision and understanding. Such an environment is approximated in parts of the American Southwest, where rock art pilgrims experience the objects of their quest in a harsh, but spiritually charged environment.

This process of pilgrimage leads to a very personal experience of the three-way relationship between the desired object (the rock art itself), the world, and the consciousness of self. In this moment of contemplation and heightened awareness it may be suggested that a form of initiation takes place in which one is (however temporarily) changed. Eliade writes that "in philosophical terms, initiation is equivalent to an ontological mutation of the existential condition. The novice emerges from his ordeal a totally different being: he has become another."[42] The notion of initiation contains the ideas of symbolic death and rebirth, and of an irrevocable transition into a new way of life. In "primitive" societies the shaman and medicine man mediate the initiatory experience through dreams, visions, and trances. In contemporary society the artist performs an important part of that "other-worldly" experience. While profound initiatory experiences take place infrequently, life is composed of rituals, such as weekly communion for the church-goer or regular museum attendance for the "true believer" in art, that commemorate or reinforce the original initiation.

The spiritual world view of all religious thought rests on the unquestioned reality of what we call myth, ritual, and magic. The shaman uses these concepts to evoke the transcendent realities of the cosmos and the links between man and sacred things.

> Myth provides the ideological content for a sacred form of behavior. Ritual brings the creative events of the beginning of time to life and enables them to be repeated here and now, in the present. The ordinary reality of everyday life recedes and is superceded by the reality of ritual drama. What was once possible and operative in the beginning of time becomes possible once more and can exert its influence anew.[43]

Religious thought calls us to recreate the oneness with God at the beginning of time (the Garden of Eden). Similarly, the special aura of rock art sites implies the need to recreate the wholeness, innocence, and "magic" that we imagine existing at the beginning of human history.

The motif of the expulsion from the Garden symbolizes the placelessness of modern man. John Haines has written that "it is land, *place,* that makes people [but] few of us these days are really residents anywhere, in the deep sense of that term."[44] It is this profound need for a sense of place and orientation that both spiritual pursuits and much contemporary art seek to satisfy. Religion provides orientation by changing the way we perceive space and place.

> For religious (i.e. pre-technological) man, space is not homogenous. . . . This spatial non-homogeneity finds expression in the experience of opposition between space that is sacred—the only *real* and *real-ly* existing space—and all other space, the formless expanse surrounding it. . . .
>
> The religious experience of the non-homogeneity of space is a primordial experience [corresponding] to a founding of the world . . . it is the break effected in space that allows the world to be constituted, because it reveals the fixed point, the central axis for all future orientation. . . . Nothing can begin, nothing can be *done,* without a previous orientation. . . . *If the world is to be lived in,* it must be *founded*—and no world can come to birth in the chaos of the homogeneity and relativity of profane space. The discovery or projection of a fixed point . . . is equivalent to the creation of the world.[45]

Similarly, modern artists seek a fundamental sense of orientation through their understanding of rock art and the creation of their own expressive works. In both cases, this sense of place may encompass several kinds of orientation: geographic (to major topographical features, or the cardinal points), astronomical (to the sun, moon, or solstices), or spiritual (the marked spot as a center of the world or universe). In the contemporary appreciation of ancient rock art, these sites are understood to have an aura or power that can magnetize the sensitive person to a kind of psychic "true north." For contemporary viewers, each rock art site comes to suggest itself as the center of an ancient, sacred realm in which man and nature were one. They suggest a time when all language was poetry and man possessed the strength of magic.

The subjectivity of this vision suggests that all our images of the world are ultimately expressions of the self. In his book *The Minimal Self,* Christopher Lasch describes the state of the modern self as one of rootlessness, without a clear sense of the past or confidence in the future. This state is characterized by protective irony, emotional disengagement, a sense of powerlessness, and a fascination with extreme situations. Lasch attributes a significant part of modern man's placelessness and sense of unreality to the mass-production, commodity-based nature of modern society. In his view, dependence, disorientation, and passivity naturally result from the frenzied pace of change and the relativity of values common to the free-market system. As Marx wrote in 1848,

> constant revolutionizing of production, uninterrupted disturbance of all social conditions, everlasting uncertainty and agitation distinguish the bourgeois epoch from all earlier ones. All fixed, fast-frozen relations, with their train of ancient and venerable prejudices and opinions, are swept away, all new-formed ones become antiquated before they can ossify. All that is solid melts into the air, all that is holy is profaned. . . .[46]

In Lasch's view such societies encourage the perception of the world as a mirror in which we see the projection of our own fears and desires. The self, unsure of its own outlines, seeks to define itself in the most basic and fundamental terms and to feel at one with the world. Art and religion are both ways of restoring or recreating the deep-seated, mythical feeling of original wholeness that Lasch attributes to our longing for the contentment of the womb. Thus, both the aggressive drive for dominance of the world and the passive desire for a magic merger with it represent an unconscious desire for the "undifferentiated equilibrium of the prenatal state, and both, moreover, reject psychological maturation in favor of regression, the 'feminine' longing for symbiosis is no less so than the solipsistic 'masculine' drive for absolute mastery."[47]

Lasch feels that an exclusive emphasis on mysticism and spirituality ultimately belies the complex nature of human existence. For him, the selfhood that arises from a consciousness that includes *self*-consciousness is the awareness of man's contradictory place in the natural order of things. It is necessary to accept our separation from nature which, by itself, does not offer us a home. "The innocence of nature is harmony without freedom."[48] The self-consciousness that distinguishes us from other species makes us aware of that crucial tension between our dependence on nature and our abilities to transcend it. Humanity wavers constantly between arrogant pride and a humiliating sense of weakness.

> Both the champions and the critics of the rational ego turn their backs on what remains valuable in the Western, Judeo-Christian tradition of individualism . . . : the definition of selfhood as tension, division, conflict. As Niebuhr pointed out, attempts to ease an uneasy conscious take the form of a denial of man's divided nature.[49]

The notion of a pristine original state, like the biblical Eden, is deeply woven into the fabric of modern thought. Marilynne Robinson has noted that

> while we have no sense of history, we are enchanted by a myth of history, a truly venerable fable, which goes like this: Once the world was as it ought to be, then came the Catastrophe, after which we have toiled in twilight, lost and downcast. No one knows how old that story is, but it has never been more passionately believed than it is now.[50]

Robinson asserts that mythical thinking embodies our need to believe that what is valued is, in fact, *natural,* and would be true today but for the flaw of the Fall. Through such thinking we express a deep emotional bond with an image of the past, "but we do not express a sense of history." History, by contrast, "is slow, slovenly, bloody, disheveled—our authentic ancestor, in whose lineaments we can clearly discover all our vices. . . ."[51] But the notion of a fundamental loss or deterioration is central to contemporary mythic thinking. "The idea at the heart of modernism is that once beauty and meaning blossomed in the meadows of experience. . . . A premodern consciousness was, presumably, as sound and shapely as a good pear."[52]

While this Romanticizing attitude toward the past distorts what some would call the "objective" content of history, it expresses deep and profound truths about the nature of human memory and understanding. At any given time we inevitably remember that which serves our present needs. "To remember is to distort, no matter whether the distortions tend to turn to nightmares or sweet dreams. If memory is the conservation of time, even more it is its betrayal."[53] Ideological and sacred histories weave past, present, and future into a symmetric, meaningful, and poetic whole that denies the ambiguities, disappointments, and tedium of secular history. As Malraux suggested, if "History transforms Destiny to awareness, Art transforms time to freedom—a freedom asserted in metamorphoses, which renew the past."[54] Art and Myth rescue a sense of human value and narrative closure from the frightening vastness of time. They provide a kind of poetic dispensation from secular history in which fabulous beginnings, a mythic wholeness, and sacred traditions confirm a sense of cultural and individual worth. This past is deeply imbued with the essence of eternity, simplicity, purity, and effortless beauty, while evoking the passion of creation and the innocent joy of new life.

This process of forgetting in order to remember is central to our search for ultimate meanings. However, it clearly contains both contradictions and dilemmas. "To expect that poetry, and only poetry, will redeem the time . . . is to expect a poeticized politics that moves toward a totalitarian end to all true poetry."[55] In the ideal holistic world of the past/future, whose values—from those currently in circulation and contention—will rule? It is worth considering that complete cultural singularity negates our treasured notions of freedom, individuality, and difference, and thus the basic premises of modern art. Our current skepticism toward all claims to authority gives us a real, if problematic freedom. How, then, do we unlearn the lessons of skepticism and regain faith? In fact, it is perhaps impossible for us, in a society of competing ideas and claims to authority, to fully understand the nature of the faith we attribute to primal man. It may be suggested that ancient peoples believed in certain "religious" and "spiritual" concepts in something like the way we "believe" in gravity: that is, as a constant and unquestioned—albeit invisible—*reality*. Paul Shepard has written that the aesthetics of landscape were derived from science and analytic vision; "scenery arose when man withdrew from the picture and turned to look at it."[56] If that is true, how do we surrender our objective view in order to step back into the picture/world? And finally, although we term these petroglyphs and pictographs primal "art" are they, in fact, anything like works of modern art in terms of ideology, historical causality or intentionality? How can we make them "ours" without hopelessly distorting their "actual" meaning? Clifford Geertz writes that

> whatever use the imaginative productions of other peoples— predecessors, ancestors, or distant cousins—can have for our moral lives, then, it cannot be to simplify them. The image of the past (or the primitive, or the classic, or the exotic) as a source of remedial wisdom, a prosthetic corrective to a damaged spiritual life—an image that has governed a good deal of humanist thought and education—is mischievous because it leads us to expect that our uncertainties will be reduced by access to thought-worlds constructed along lines alternative to our own, when in fact they will be multiplied . . . the growth in range a powerful sensibility gains from an encounter with another one, as powerful or more, comes only at the expense of its inward ease.[57]

And, on the surface, it seems that it is just this sort of inward ease that we are attempting to regain.

These complex questions suggest, in part, the "irrationalities" of faith that underlie all world views, secular and sacred. Our contemporary understanding of these ancient rock art sites is guided by a deeply utopian and other-worldly vision that is a fundamental part of the modernist tradition. And despite the inevitable, "logical" dilemmas accompanying *all* utopian visions, this stance represents an important set of values and attitudes. By honestly perceiving these marks in our own cultural image these artists express their faith in what today's art can and should be. Their images are deeply moral visions conveying a profound respect for the evidence of time, the primacy of culture, and the grandeur of the earth. They offer an implicit critique of our own moral relativism and spiritual malaise, while celebrating the transcendent power of human expression and imagination.

In their interpretation of these ancient marks, these photographers succeed in making art both about the world and about art itself. This dual awareness acknowledges our artistic self-consciousness as well as our longing for a transparent rendering of—and communion with—the things outside us. And, by recording artifacts of (presumed) communal belief, these artists reflect their own desire for a contemporary art that is equally central to life. By celebrating the primacy of the creative and expressive act, these photographers suggest the timelessness and naturalness of their own artistic endeavor. Such self-justification seems unfortunately necessary in a society which generally considers art as either trivial entertainment or impenetrable self-absorption and, in either case, as irrelevant to daily concerns. By contrast, these photographers' works are, at root, about the fundamental ways we think about each other and live in our world, every day of our lives.

In the act of contemplating these images of formal simplicity, mythic meaning and cultural primacy we, as sympathetic viewers, find ourselves reflected in them. We meditate on their mute forms and merge past, present, and future into a charged Now of heightened awareness. The burden of alienated selfhood is lessened by a feeling for our individual smallness, and our relationship to larger forces. And a sense of reverential terror may be inferred from the sublime isolation of so many of these sites, warning us of our own power to remove ourselves—if not all our traces—from the face of the earth. In their ability to reflect vitally important facets of our current notions of art, selfhood, and spirituality, these ancient marks become the most modern of Readymades. And they reveal the poignant truth of Proust's observation that "the only true paradises are the paradises we have lost."[58]

NOTES

1. My use of the term *modernism* in this essay probably requires some clarification. By ascribing modernist sensibilities to these contemporary photographers, I am *not* marking them as conservative or reactionary artists in a "postmodern" culture. We are still very much in the modern era, although "High Modernism," as a style, describes a particular historical movement (by some accounts, 1885–1925). The modern mind has roots in Classical thought and grew rapidly in the Scientific Revolution and Age of Enlightenment. It is characterized by a skepticism toward traditional claims to authority, a heightened sense of individuality, and a notion of progress coupled with a need for periodic renewal. Every modernist movement has rejected certain aspects of an earlier style's basic presumption of reality. These contested aspects of reality have varied from one artistic paradigm shift to another, and have included the basic nature of visual, narrative, psychological, or political experience. Each of these shifts draws much of its power by excluding competing facets of reality from consideration, and thereby establishes itself as the whole of valued experience. As such, these movements are important reflections of time-bound cultural values and beliefs. The need to perceive oneself as fundamentally different and more advanced than one's predecessors (while, at the same time, harkening back to an even *earlier* era) is, to my mind, an intrinsically modernist trait. The loudly proclaimed rupture of the postmodern from a discredited modernist past is unconvincing, since the need for such disavowals is basic to modernism's paradoxical tradition of revolution. Thus, my emphasis here is on continuities rather than disjunctions.

2. Richard Ellman and Charles Feidelson, Jr., *The Modern Tradition: Backgrounds of Modern Literature* (New York: Oxford University Press, 1965), p. 9.

3. Bertrand Russell, *A History of Western Philosophy* (New York: Simon and Schuster, 1945, 1972), p. 683.

4. Friedrich Nietzsche, *The Birth of Tragedy* (1872), in *The Modern Tradition*, p. 549.

5. *Ibid.*, p. 551.

6. *Ibid.*, p. 550.

7. *The Modern Tradition*, p. 446.

8. Ernst Cassirer, *Language and Myth* (1925), in *The Modern Tradition*, p. 636.

9. Paul Gauguin, quoted by Andre Fontainas (1899), in Herschel B. Chipp, *Theories of Modern Art* (Berkeley: University of California Press, 1968), p. 73.

10. G. Albert Aurier, "Essay on a New Method of Criticism" (1890–93), in Chipp, p. 88.

11. Aurier, "Symbolism in Painting: Paul Gauguin" (1891), in Chipp, p. 92–93.

12. Bram Dijkstra, *Cubism, Stieglitz and the Early Poetry of William Carlos Williams* (Princeton: Princeton University Press, 1969), pp. 102–3.

13. James Ensor, from a speech on 22 December 1923, in Chipp, p. 111.

14. Chipp, p. 367.

15. Wassily Kandinsky, "The Effects of Color" (1911), in Chipp, p. 153.

16. Piet Mondrian, "Plastic Art and Pure Plastic Art" (1937), in Chipp, p. 361.

17. Marsden Hartley, "Art—and the Personal Life" (1928), in Chipp, p. 526.

18. Essay written by Weston in leaflet (1934) for Los Angeles Museum; quoted in Ben Maddow, *Edward Weston: Seventy Photographs* (Boston: New York Graphic Society, 1978), p. 99.

19. Brancusi, undated aphorisms, in Chipp, p. 365.

20. *Ibid.*, p. 127.

21. *Ibid.*, p. 273.

22. Franz Marc, aphorisms (1914–15), in Chipp, p. 180.

23. Mark Rothko, "The Romantics Were Prompted" (1947), in Chipp, p. 548.

24. Wassily Kandinsky, "On the Problems of Form" (1912), in Chipp, p. , 166.
25. F. T. Marinetti, "The Exhibitors to the Public" (1912), in Chipp, p. 294.
26. Kasimir Malevich, "Suprematism" (1927), in Chipp, p. 344.
27. Giorgio de Chirico, "Mystery and Creation" (1913), in Chipp, p. 401.
28. Adolf Gottlieb and Mark Rothko, "Statement" (1943), in Chipp, p. 544.
29. Robert Motherwell, in "Symposium: What Abstract Art Means to Me" (1953), in Chipp, p. 563.
30. Barnett Newman, "The First Man Was an Artist" (1947), in Chipp, p. 551.
31. *Ibid.*, p. 552.
32. Suzi Gablik, "Minimalism," in Nikos Stangos, ed., *Concepts of Modern Art* (New York: Harper and Row, 1981), p. 253.
33. Patrick J. Keane, "Yeats's Counter-Enlightenment," *Salmagundi* 68–69 (Fall 1985–Winter 1986): 141.
34. Alain Robbe-Grillet, "Dehumanizing Nature," in *The Modern Tradition*, pp. 365, 370.
35. Morris Berman, *The Reenchantment of the World* (New York: Bantam Books, 1984), p. 82.
36. Jamake Highwater, *The Primal Mind* (New York: New American Library, 1981), p. 39.
37. *Ibid.*, p. 41.
38. *Ibid.*, pp. 210–11.
39. M. L. von Franz, "The Process of Individuation," in Carl G. Jung, et. al., *Man and his Symbols* (New York: Dell Publishing Co., 1964), pp. 221, 224.
40. Mircea Eliade, *The Quest: History and Meaning in Religion* (Chicago: University of Chicago Press, 1969), p. 41.
41. Paul Shepard, *Man in the Landscape* (New York: Alfred A. Knopf, 1967), p. 43.
42. Eliade, p. 112.
43. Lauri Honko, "The Problem of Defining Myth," in Alan Dundes, ed., *Sacred Narrative: Readings in the Theory of Myth* (Berkeley: University of California Press, 1984), p. 51.
44. John Haines, *Living Off the Country: Essays on Poetry and Place* (Ann Arbor: University of Michigan Press, 1981), p. 7.
45. Mircea Eliade, *The Sacred and the Profane,* pp. 20–22; quoted in Nicholas J. Capasso, "Environmental Art: Strategies for Reorientation in Nature," *Arts Magazine* (January 1985):73.
46. Karl Marx and Friedrich Engels, *The Communist Manifesto* (1848), in *The Modern Tradition,* p. 331.
47. Christopher Lasch, *The Minimal Self* (New York: W.W. Norton and Company, 1984), p. 246.
48. *Ibid.*, p. 257.
49. *Ibid.*, p. 258.
50. Marilynne Robinson, "Writers and the Nostalgic Fallacy," *New York Times Book Review,* October 13, 1985, p. 1.
51. *Ibid.*, p. 34.
52. *Ibid.*, p. 34.
53. Erich Heller, "Nietzsche's Terror: Time and the Inarticulate," *Salmagundi,* p. 83.
54. Malraux, cited in Wylie Sypher, "Aesthetic of Doom: Malraux," *Salmagundi,* p. 154.
55. John P. Sisk, "Poetry and the Forgetting of History," *Salmagundi,* p. 75.
56. Shepard, p. 124.
57. Clifford Geertz, *Local Knowledge: Further Essays in Interpretive Anthropology* (New York: Basic Books, 1983), pp. 44–45.
58. Proust, cited in Stephen Kern, *The Culture of Time and Space 1880–1918* (Cambridge: Harvard University Press, 1983), p. 49.

About the Contributors

Linda Connor has taught photography at the San Francisco Art Institute since 1969. A book of her photographs is entitled *Solos* (Apeiron, 1979).

Keith Davis is curator of the Fine Arts Collections at Hallmark Cards, Inc., in Kansas City and the author of *Désiré Charnay: Expeditionary Photographer* (University of New Mexico Press, 1981).

Rick Dingus is assistant professor of photography at Texas Tech University in Lubbock. He is the author of *The Photographic Artifacts of Timothy O'Sullivan* (University of New Mexico Press, 1982).

Steve Fitch is lecturer in the Visual Studies Program at Princeton University and the author of *Diesels and Dinosaurs* (Long Run Press, 1976).

Lucy R. Lippard is the author of thirteen books on contemporary art, among them *Overlay: Contemporary Art and the Art of Prehistory* (Pantheon, 1983).

John Pfahl, formerly professor of photography at the Rochester Institute of Technology, is currently based in Buffalo, New York. Books of his work include *Altered Landscapes* (Friends of Photography, 1979) and the forthcoming *Arcadia Revisited: Photographs of the Niagara River* (University of New Mexico Press) and *Picture Windows* (New York Graphic Society).

Charles Roitz is professor of photography at the University of Colorado at Boulder.

Polly Schaafsma is an artist and a research associate of the Museum of New Mexico. She is the author of *Indian Rock Art of the Southwest* (School of American Research and University of New Mexico Press, 1980).

Marks in Place
Contemporary Responses to Rock Art

Designed by Barbara Jellow
Typography in VIP Century Oldstyle
by the University of New Mexico Printing Plant
Printed by DNP (America), Inc.
Printed in Japan